What people are saying about The [...]
(formerly Is There a Moose [...]

"As our marriages and our homes di[...]
finger at others to assign blame. It is refreshing to read *The [...]
Incorrect Wife*, which is focused on our own responsibility to be who
God has called us to be. Three cheers for Nancy Cobb and Connie
Grigsby! Their book gives more than just answers; it gives truth and
hope. It is a book that I look forward to sharing with my own
daughters."

ANNE GRAHAM LOTZ, SPEAKER AND AUTHOR OF
JUST GIVE ME JESUS

"Practical, fun, and absolutely life changing. You'll laugh, but you
will also be inspired. It's perfect for newlyweds, but also for those,
like me, who have been married a long time and have wonderful
marriages. I can't recommend this manual for wives from Nancy
Cobb and Connie Grigsby highly enough."

DEE BRESTIN, SPEAKER AND AUTHOR OF
THE FRIENDSHIPS OF WOMEN

"The many 'how to's' found within *The Politically Incorrect Wife* will
show you how to gently unwrap the gift that is your mate! We've
been blessed to read most of the current books on marriage, and
this is one of the very best!"

BOB AND DIANE REILLY, MARRIAGE MINISTRIES
INTERNATIONAL, COHOSTS OF *MARRIAGE MATTERS*

"*The Politically Incorrect Wife* is a must-have book for every pastor's
library. Nancy and Connie's sound biblical teaching and Spirit-filled
insights can benefit every pastor engaged in premarital and marriage
counseling."

REVEREND KENNETH LETTERMAN, FAITH PRESBYTERIAN
CHURCH, GERMANTOWN, TENNESSEE

"I am the recipient and blessed husband of a wife who applied (and
still does) the principles enumerated in this excellent and very practical book. They have marvelously changed my life on this earth
and for eternity."

LARRY WRIGHT, FOUNDER, ABUNDANT LIFE, INC.

"Get out your highlighter and read this book...you won't be disappointed!"

KENT JULIAN, YOUTH MINISTER

And now, How to Get Your Husband to Talk to You:

"Don't miss this book! It's fun, realistic, smart, helpful—on every page. Mind you, I don't have any feelings about it. We're talking straight problem-solving here.... Think of it as an armchair travel book, an interplanetary cruise, a Grunt-English dictionary. Think of it as 'your husband is a TV,' and you—for once—have the remote."

DAVID KOPP, COAUTHOR WITH HEATHER HARPHAM KOPP
OF *LOVE STORIES GOD TOLD* AND
PRAYING THE BIBLE FOR YOUR MARRIAGE

"Nancy and Connie have filled this book with wise and wonderful counsel on understanding the differences between how men and women communicate. *How to Get Your Husband to Talk to You* is a treasure of personal experiences, tried and true ideas, and seasoned insights on marriage. My husband and I have been married almost forty-four years, and how I wish I'd had this book in the early years! Whether you're a new bride or have been married for many years, following the advice in this book can greatly improve your marriage. You may even fall in love with your husband all over again!"

SHEILA CRAGG, CREATOR OF WWW.WOMANSWALK.COM

"*How to Get Your Husband to Talk to You* addresses an age-old question asked by all women in love. Connie and Nancy offer a fresh reminder to honor and accept your man. You'll learn how to frame your words, diminish your details, and acknowledge your differences. The authors' warm, story-vignette style of writing makes this book an easy, quick read."

DONNA OTTO, AUTHOR OF *THE GENTLE ART OF
MENTORING*, FOUNDER OF HOMEMAKERS BY CHOICE

The *Best* thing I ever did *for* my marriage

NANCY COBB & CONNIE GRIGSBY

Multnomah® Publishers *Sisters, Oregon*

THE BEST THING I EVER DID FOR MY MARRIAGE
published by Multnomah Publishers, Inc.

© 2003 by Nancy Cobb and Connie Grigsby
International Standard Book Number: 1-59052-199-4

Cover design by Kevin Keller/DesignConcepts
Cover images by Digital Vision and EyeWire

Multnomah is a trademark of Multnomah Publishers, Inc.,
and is registered in the U.S. Patent and Trademark Office.
The colophon is a trademark of Multnomah Publishers, Inc.

For information:
MULTNOMAH PUBLISHERS, INC. • P.O. BOX 1720 • SISTERS, OR 97759

Library of Congress Cataloging-in-Publication Data

Cobb, Nancy, 1938-
  The best thing I ever did for my marriage / by Nancy Cobb and Connie Grigsby.
      p. cm.
Includes bibliographical references.
  ISBN 1-59052-199-4 (pbk.)
  1. Wives—Religious life. 2. Wives—Conduct of life. 3. Marriage—Religious
aspects—Christianity. I. Grigsby, Connie. II. Title.

BV4528.15.C625 2003
248.8'435—dc21

                                    2003008419

03 04 05 06 07 08—10 9 8 7 6 5 4 3 2 1 0

To our precious families and friends,

who so willingly and generously

shared their hearts in this book.

Thank you!

And to every woman out there

who is committed to pleasing God

in her marriage and with her life.

Press on!

NANCY & CONNIE

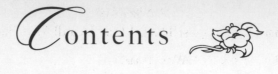ontents

section five
Refined by Fire

section six
My Cup Runneth Over

epilogue
Where You Don't Want to Live

Foreword

Less than a year ago, I was in a recording studio with Nancy Cobb and Connie Grigsby, discussing their book *How to Get Your Husband to Talk to You*. Since I operate a marriage ministry, it was the highest honor for me to interview these ladies, who have nearly seventy years of combined marriage experience. We laughed a lot that day. And Nancy and Connie shared some great stories about learning to communicate with their husbands and make the most of their differences.

And different they are!

Connie's husband likes to go skydiving for a good time, while she'd rather drink tea on the porch. (Incidentally, in her efforts to "relate" to her husband, Connie nearly killed the two of them while learning to fly an airplane.) Nancy's husband has a unique knack for "telling it like it is," even when it comes to discussing his wife's weight (not an area most men would want to discuss). It's hard to believe that any couple could make it through these kinds of differences!

The reality is, when two people join hands in marriage, there's a good chance their differences will collide like two gasoline trucks on the interstate. Many couples ignore their differences until the damage seems insurmountable. You may be someone who went into marriage with great dreams for the things you and your spouse would accomplish together—only to see them beaten down by the battles of life. But there is hope. Your marriage is one of the greatest tools God has given you to minister to others—even if its hasn't been a smooth road.

Nancy and Connie are inordinately competent at helping women understand their role in marriage, and I guarantee you'll be encouraged by what you read here. These stories share the hearts of women who have gone before you—both the good and the bad situations. Take advantage of this "history book" and avoid many of the struggles that can weigh down a marriage. It has been said that a sign of maturity is the ability to learn from the mistakes of others. Pore over this book and learn from the mistakes of those who have gone before you! Be encouraged by the wealth of teaching and discover how to apply these principles to your own marriage. You will be blessed!

Dennis Rainey
President, FamilyLife

Acknowledgments

*T*o the gracious women who shared their stories in this book. Without you, there would be no book! We are deeply grateful. May you be blessed beyond measure.

To Renee DeLoriea, who has walked with us from the idea stage of this book to its release. What a delightful journey it has been! You are far more than an editor to us.

To Don Jacobson and all the team in Sisters, who took a risk on us five years ago. Our wonder never ceases at being a part of the Multnomah family.

To Wes and Ray for their faithful love and support as we continue our writing partnership. We love you! Also, to our beloved children, who love us regardless of what we do or whether we write! Each of you is a gift from God.

To our loyal friends who pray for us. As Oswald Chambers said, "Prayer does not equip us for greater works—prayer is the greater work." Thank you for your greater work.

Most of all, thanks be to God. To Him alone be the glory!

Introduction

When a woman marries, she carries with her the hopes and dreams she has tenderly nurtured ever since she was a little girl. Yet so often, these hopes and dreams are dashed within a few short years of the wedding—if even that long!

Her Prince Charming may not even notice that his bride's dreams are going up in smoke. In fact, he may think everything is perfectly okay! When she tries to talk to him about the situation, he either wants to fix "her" problem or change the subject entirely. Neither option does much for getting things back on track, at least for her.

Before long she begins to shut down emotionally. Now, instead of nursing hopes and dreams, she nurses a wounded spirit. Realizing that something is going on but unsure what it is, he begins to withdraw as well. Soon they become like two strangers living under the same roof, simply coexisting. What was once a warm, fulfilling relationship is now barely sucking in enough oxygen to survive.

Sound familiar?

You're about to embark on an eye-opening journey that we believe you'll walk away from feeling hopeful and inspired. The women in this book have walked in your shoes! With refreshing honesty and insight, they share the struggles in their marriages and what got them on track again. And the masks have been dropped! Topics that are rarely talked about are openly discussed with complete candor.

We didn't know what to expect when we sent out invitations to well-known and everyday women asking them the best thing they ever did for their marriage. But the stories came pouring in! Many of the contributors shocked us with their willingness to reveal their hidden sins, flaws, and wounds. The thrilling element in every single story is how God Himself intervened in each of their marriages. And just as thrilling is knowing that God still intervenes in marriages today.

Here's a sneak peek at some of the issues that will be addressed:

- **Emotional isolation**—*now* this husband bemoans the fact that there will be no marriages in heaven!
- **When he's fallen out of love with you**—learn how to avoid years of bitterness, anger, and depression.
- **The miraculous benefits of forgiveness**—it frees you to become the real you.
- **Moms-in-law**—Deannie and Diane will have you laughing out loud.
- **Conflict resolution**—if you don't resolve it, sparks will fly, all right, but not the right kind!
- **Failing miserably and feeling miserable?**—Brenda was…learn what change made all the difference.
- **Trying to do it all?**—what a relief to discover you don't have to.
- **Do you think sex is overrated?**—brace yourself for the chapter called "This Will Be Your Husband's Favorite Chapter!"
- **Does your husband feel your worth is directly proportional to your weight?**—get ready for the chapter called "Politically Incorrect"!

- The pain and heartache of adultery—discover how to protect your marriage.
- Can God resurrect something from a pile of ashes?—absolutely!
- And much more!

Regardless of whether every chapter applies to you or not, we think you'll be encouraged and heartened. Each chapter offers insight to help you build a stronger marriage, while sharing inspirational truths about God's design for your life.

Maybe you're one of the many women who feels that if only her husband would change, she'd be happy. What woman hasn't thought that at some point? The truth is that you can't force another person to change, but you *can* work on you. And when a woman is willing to work on herself, the results are astonishing.

This book isn't about trying harder to be a good wife; it's about surrendering your marriage—and yourself—to its Inventor. Only God can completely meet your needs when others fail.

As you close the final pages of this book, we hope you'll feel like you made fifty new friends and witnessed the hand of God in each of their marriages. What you may discover as well is that dashed hopes and dreams have a way of making their way back into a woman's heart…when God steps in!

Cold Hearts Can Be Warmed Again

Been living with an iceberg for a heart?
These women were!
Discover how cold hearts can be warmed,
and see how futility and hopelessness
can be transformed into joy, wonder,
and much surprise when a woman
embraces God's best for her life.

When Your Heart Is Empty

What to Do When the Feelings Are Gone

SUE WRIGHT
ABUNDANT LIFE, INC.

t was a warm evening in June, and my (Connie) family and I were attending a family camp in Horn Creek, Colorado. All two hundred participants were mesmerized by what the speaker was sharing about his marriage.

"Folks, it wasn't a matter of if we got divorced; it was a matter of when. It's just that neither one of us had gotten around to it yet. That's how bad our marriage had become. We were about as hopeless as it gets."

Larry Wright's words shocked me. I'd been watching him and his wife, Sue, throughout the week and couldn't help but notice how at home they seemed with one another. There was a sense of comfort—even tenderness—visible in the way they interacted. A person never would've guessed that they'd been anywhere near separation or divorce.

How I longed for this same closeness in my own marriage! At the time, Wes and I were quite unhappy—our marriage had grown

*distant and cold. Not only were we not at home with one another;
being together was downright uncomfortable and awkward.*

*But over the next several days, I learned that God can work
miracles when a woman purposes to live a life that is pleasing to
Him. Prepare to be encouraged as you read Sue's account of the
miracle that took place in her heart—and in her marriage—when
she decided to allow God to step into the marriage relationship.*

Larry and I met on a blind date in college. We were married
three months later. Each of us had this idea that the other person would make us happy for the rest of our lives. It didn't
take many months to discover that our idea was a little off! I
decided that the solution to our unhappiness was for Larry to
change.

Larry's home situation growing up wasn't ideal—he basically raised himself—so he didn't have a clue about what a
husband and father was supposed to do. I, on the other hand,
came from a very loving family and had a great relationship
with my father. I expected Larry and me to have the same
kind of close relationship.

Not only were Larry's and my backgrounds different; our
goals were different as well. After college, we moved to
Arizona, and he got a job as a disc jockey at a rock 'n' roll station. His goal was to become the number one disc jockey in
Phoenix, and it didn't take him long to get there. My goal was
to raise our three beautiful daughters and have a wonderful
family life.

But a funny thing happens on the way to success: You are
thrown into the party world, and when you're under such
pressure to be number one, you have to do something to
relax. Larry found that relaxation by spending time in bars. I

never knew for sure when he would come home. But when he did, he was a mess and I wasn't much better. Our life together began to crumble, and we didn't know what to do about it. Friends and family were quick to suggest divorce, but I was against that. We had all the things the world said would make us happy: family, success, money, and lots of material things. Yet I was totally empty, and our relationship was deteriorating.

About this time, my mom—at the age of fifty-eight—overdosed on sleeping pills and killed herself. She had reached a point where she felt that her life had no purpose—she had raised her family and helped run the family business and felt there was nothing left for her. That tragic event caused me to start questioning why I was here. Was I here just to raise a family? Was there a greater purpose to life than I was seeing? *I'm not going to make it past the age of thirty-one if there's not more to life than this*, I thought. I wanted out.

But at this low point God began to draw me to Himself. He showed me that the emptiness in my heart couldn't be filled by my husband or by anything else in this world. That emptiness was a God-shaped vacuum created *by Him* and *for Him*. I came to understand that I was a lost sinner in need of a Savior and that Jesus loved me so much that He died on the cross for my sins. My part was to accept His love and forgiveness and give Him my life. I took that step and have never been the same since.

I would love to say that everything changed from that moment on. But it didn't. I was still married to Larry! My prayer had always been, *Lord, change him, because he obviously is the problem.* Was I in for a surprise! You see, when you come into a personal relationship with God, He takes your eyes off everyone else, and you begin to see yourself in a whole new way. Being able to truly see yourself begins with having a teachable spirit and a desire for change in your life. As God revealed things to me, I began to see the situation with my husband entirely differently. I saw what a nag I had become and how unhappy and critical I was.

And because of Larry's drinking, I had reached a point where I didn't even like him. He was a failure at home, which I pointed out to him constantly, so he never came home. He was accepted at the bars and at work, so that's where he spent all his time. Why come home to failure and criticism?

I had to do something! And what I did turned out to be the hardest yet most important thing I ever did for my marriage: I gave my husband completely to the Lord. God loved him more than I did, and He wanted that love to be demonstrated through me.

On the day I accepted Christ, I discovered that His love never ceases. His love is constant and He is full of compassion. That love is never based on my performance. It is given freely and has nothing to do with feelings. That same love in Christ Jesus was now in me, too. All I had to do was be willing to forgive my husband as Christ had forgiven me and let go of all the bitterness and anger.

Because of my anger and unhappiness, I had stopped showing love to my husband. But I now recognized my need to change. Love is action, and I began to love my husband as Christ wanted me to—even though I didn't feel like it. I learned that love is not a feeling! It is an act of the will. And with that change, Larry saw a peace, joy, and love in me he had never seen before. When you do loving things for your husband, the feelings *do* come back. What a mess we had been in! We were two selfish individuals looking to the other for happiness. God took hold of my heart and then with His love touched the heart of Larry Wright.

Larry became a new man. And with that change, God gave Larry a wonderful gift of teaching and used him in ways I never could've imagined. He also restored to us a love for one another that was so awesome and that lasted for forty-six years (and we didn't think we could make it for seven!). Over the last thirty years, we have taught and helped others understand that with God nothing is impossible. He can take broken lives and hearts and make something out of nothing. When you become secure in God's love, you can then reach out and love the unlovable, expecting nothing in return.

On October 7, 2001, my darling went home to be with the Lord. I miss him so much and long for the day when we will be together again. I thank the Lord for His marvelous plan for our lives. It has been a blast!

We all have the choice to obey God's Word, and when we're willing to trust Him with the results, amazing things can happen.

The week following Larry's death, Focus on the Family devoted its entire Friday program to his memory by playing a tape recorded years before. As founders of Abundant Life, Inc., Sue and Larry had been guests numerous times.

As I listened, I was reminded of a conversation I'd had with Larry a few years before. He had called one night about writing an endorsement for our book The Politically Incorrect Wife.

A few days after our conversation, his endorsement landed on my desk. It read: "I am the recipient and blessed husband of a wife who applied (and still does) the principles enumerated in this excellent and very practical book. They have marvelously changed my life on this earth and for eternity."

Larry Wright's life was changed—for eternity—by his wife's influence. Sue's decision to love her husband unconditionally led Larry to a relationship with Christ. And because of that, the abilities that had vaulted him to the top of the disc jockey profession were used to impact thousands for the Lord—all because of a woman who was willing to change.

Does the way you treat your husband make him want to know more of God?

Two Strangers Living Under the Same Roof

Emotional Isolation Chills a Home Like Little Else

S U Z I   M c D U F F E E

uzi is my (Nancy) best friend. We met in 1981 at a Bible study taught by Anne Graham Lotz. We began the study the same year and came to a saving relationship with Christ in the same month. Seven years after we met, we became involved in ministry together. Her investment in my life has been enormous. This book could not be large enough to mention the many acts of service and kindness she has shown me. When I think of a woman who most exhibits the fruits of the Spirit, I think of Suzi.

As kids, one of the delights of our Christmas holidays was receiving special gift boxes of freshly picked fruit from Florida and Oregon from our father. We feasted on these treats all through the holidays and joked that those luscious fruits were a little taste of heaven. It wasn't until much later in life that I learned that my heavenly Father has provided fruit even sweeter than anything my family had shared together at Christmas. The special gift from God is spiritual fruit that lasts forever.

My friendship with my husband, Curt, began on a blind date in college. From the beginning, it was as if we had always known each other, and after two years we married. We had the usual newlywed adjustments, but for the most part we delighted in each other's company. We enjoyed just being together. Over the years, God blessed us with two wonderful sons, a lovely home, and a wide circle of friends and activities. A casual observer would have said we were living the American dream and enjoying the perfect marriage. I should've been gloriously happy, but I wasn't. There was an emptiness in my heart that no amount of activity could fill.

Curt was a loving, attentive husband, but he couldn't fill that void in my life. I began to wonder, *Is this all there is to life? Why am I here? What is my purpose?* My discontent with who I was and where I was going caused me to be distant and self-focused. Before I realized it, Curt and I had become two virtual strangers living in the same house, isolated by our thoughts and emotions.

That same year a friend invited me to a Bible study. I figured that I had tried everything else in my search for contentment; why not try God's Word? On my class registration card, I wrote, "I'm joining this class so I can know God better." But after the first few weeks of study, I quickly realized that I didn't know God at all.

In October of 1981, I made a decision to ask Jesus to be my Savior and acknowledged His right to be Lord of my life, including my activities, thoughts, attitudes, and family—

especially my marriage. I put my life and my future in God's hands.

That decision changed my life more than I could have imagined. The emptiness I had felt was gradually replaced with an inner sense of joy and satisfaction I had never experienced before. Finally I had peace. I was thrilled with the change, but my husband wasn't pleased. I tried to share my newfound faith with him, but he felt threatened by this new direction in my life. His reaction was heartbreaking, so I turned to Jesus and presented my marriage to Him.

My daily prayer became, *Lord, make me the kind of wife who will be a joy to my husband all his days. Restore the vitality, intimacy, and delight in our relationship so that it is better than it ever was before. Please bring Curt into a full and intimate relationship with You so that we can share our faith together.*

As a new Christian, I was aware of the incredible power available through prayer, so I began to concentrate that prayer power on my immediate family, particularly on my husband. One of the verses I had memorized about God's gift of spiritual fruit kept running through my mind: "The fruit of the Spirit is love, joy, peace, patience, kindness, goodness, faithfulness, gentleness and self-control."[1] I knew that I hadn't consistently lived out these characteristics in my marriage relationship, but if I could, maybe Curt's reactions would be different. So I prayed that I would be able to change.

Time and again during prayer, that still, small voice of God's Spirit would prompt me to think about how to show my love and commitment to my husband. Often I would go directly from my prayer time to seeing to my husband's needs. Having experienced God's lavish love for me in Christ, I was now free to love my husband lavishly as well. I began to pray about each aspect of the spiritual fruit basket God had provided me with to see how I could best apply it to my marriage. I made a conscious choice daily to surrender to the work of the Holy Spirit, and soon His fruit began to ripen in me.

The first fruit—love—seemed simple enough to express to my husband. How often did I show Curt my love by freely giving my time to him? How sensitive had I been to his physical and emotional needs? I realized that often I was too busy with my own affairs to think about what would please him. I knew Curt wanted my attention. He loved to have me just sit with him and watch a favorite show or ride along on an errand. Slowly, as my behavior and attitude became more loving, a freshness returned to our relationship. With God's help, I had new eyes and a grateful heart to see my husband as a precious gift. It was then that I realized that my former complaining and critical spirit had robbed me—and Curt—of joy.

The fruit of peace developed in me as I learned to trust Jesus to help me overcome my tendency to worry and be anxious. A new sense of joy entered my life, and as I spent time in God's Word and in daily prayer, I found that I could stay calm and peaceful, even in life's most challenging situations. Curt and I faced job loss, cancer, starting a new business, and the care of aging parents, but instead of our marriage being torn apart, we found ourselves clinging together with a new intimacy and increasing faith.

Four of the next fruits—patience, kindness, goodness, and gentleness—took time and prayer to develop, but slowly I found my reactions changing. I learned how to wait patiently for my husband to become the man God had designed him to be. It didn't happen the way I would have planned, without any difficulties, but the result was far more than I could have imagined. God brought Curt into a full relationship of faith and began to mold his character to reflect His Son. I found myself wanting to respond to Curt with kindness and gentleness, and my prayer became, *Lord make your fruit reach perfection in both of us!*

The fruits of faithfulness and self-control developed through my service in a wonderful teaching ministry. I had come to love God's Word. And as I faithfully hid it in my heart, it became easier to live it out in my marriage. I found that I could be more self-controlled in my responses to my husband and didn't have to lash out in anger or impatience. Increasingly, I became less and less selfish—striving to please Curt instead of myself. Harmony and joy entered our marriage as never before.

My husband and I have been married thirty-five years now. I am graying and showing the signs of middle age, yet to my utter amazement my husband sees me as more beautiful and appealing than when I was a young coed of nineteen. His eyes light up when he looks at me; a smile breaks across his face as he thinks of the sweet times we have shared together. He seems to delight in my presence. How can that be explained after all these years? In one word—*Jesus*. The best thing I ever did for my marriage was to surrender my life and marriage to Christ's lordship and then unwrap His special fruit basket—full of spiritual fruits that have truly made my marriage a taste of heaven.

This story contains the key ingredients needed for a marriage that brings glory to God—the fruits of the Spirit. God is intensely interested in the condition of our marriages and invites us to pray. Often we are quick to spend time on the phone or in a restaurant with friends complaining about the state of our marriages—yet so often we fail to bring the matter to the One who created this union. Suzi prayed. God worked. And He can do the same for you.

Ask God to bring both you and your husband into a relationship with Him— and into a revitalized union with each other.

Second Chances

A Courageous Person Sees the Need for a Fresh Start—
And Then Starts Fresh

THERESA HOWELL

Years ago, I (Connie) read a fascinating story about the famous inventor Alfred Nobel. He woke up one morning to see his obituary in the newspaper. In it he was remembered for amassing a fortune with the invention of dynamite.

It was an error! It was Alfred's brother Emil who had died. But the account of Alfred's life had a profound effect on him. He wanted to be remembered for something other than figuring out a way to kill large numbers of people at once and making a lot of money in doing so.

So he initiated the Nobel Prize, saying, "Every man ought to have the chance to correct his epitaph in midstream and write a new one."

It's amazing how a marriage can be changed when one of its members decides it's time to correct the marital epitaph—and write a new one.

Very shortly after my dad died in May 2001, I began to notice that my husband, Bob, was being especially sweet and attentive to me. He complimented me like I hadn't heard in years and surprised me with romantic gestures—he sent flowers, stole me away for a night, and wrote sweet love notes. We didn't have a conversation about this "conversion" until much later because I was afraid it wasn't going to last and he'd revert back to his old way of "just getting along."

Our first twenty-five years together had been spent raising kids, but now that they were grown and on their own, it was time to see exactly what our marriage was made of. I must admit that I didn't think Bob really *liked* me. I knew he loved me, but I didn't feel we were on the same team anymore. He did his thing and I did mine. The spark had gone out of the relationship. Our faith had grown over the years, but regrettably, I showed my graciousness and love to everyone *but Bob*. In my mind, he was supposed to be perfect and didn't need any encouragement and support from me. And since I wasn't hearing any from him, I assumed he felt the same way.

So this sudden showering of compliments totally surprised me. I figured he felt sorry for me since my dad had just died. But his attention to me didn't stop; in fact, it only became more frequent and creative. At first I wasn't very receptive. I always had one eyebrow raised, wondering what his ulterior motives were. But more and more I began to see that there were none—he simply wanted to show me how much he loved me. My dad's death had caused him to realize how short life is, and he wanted to live out his promise to God to love and honor me for the rest of his life.

He began building me up, and I in turn started doing the same thing. It's amazing that when one partner starts being generous toward the other, the second partner feels drawn to do likewise. It wasn't easy at first because it felt so foreign to me. I had become proficient at put-downs and at pointing out what was wrong. But when you're being complimented for just being you, it's hard to push it away. God created us to love and be loved, and I believe that when we give love, we're most fulfilled. I was happier than I'd been in ages.

Our love blossomed into a return to our early days of courtship, when we couldn't wait to see each other. We now focused on each other's positive qualities instead of on the negative ones—and what a change it made!

We also began praying together. The power of prayer before the Almighty at the end of the day is indescribable. It is so rewarding and draws you into an intimacy with your partner and with God like nothing else can. Sometimes we're exhausted, but we look at each other, knowing that God is waiting, and we fall to our knees, thanking Him for the day and asking Him for another chance to serve Him tomorrow.

Our kids have commented on our "new" relationship, which is so encouraging. I'm thankful God gave us a second chance to model for them what a godly marriage looks like— it takes a lot of work, but it's a beautiful vocation! Only when you make Jesus the center will marriage be successful. We always try to give God the glory as we enjoy each other—we wasted so many years just tolerating each other, instead of loving each other, but now we're on the same team and it feels so good.

It's wonderful to feel "in love" with your partner again. Bob and I laugh more, hug more, and spend more time together. I *want* to be with Bob now. Our favorite line is "You're so good to me." And the other's response is "You're so easy to be good to!"

Our love continues to deepen and grow as we focus on the positive and give unselfishly—without counting the cost!

It has been a great joy to have a second chance to become one with my partner.

Theresa and Bob's daughter, Kari, was married a year ago. I (Connie) talked with her at a bridal shower a few weeks before her wedding, and she shared with me what a wonderful example her parents' marriage was to her. Surely this is sweet music to their ears.

Second chances can impact many more lives than just your own! Because Theresa's husband was willing to start over, and because she joined him, every day has taken on a fresh hue. Their four adult kids have seen what it looks like for Dad to love Mom and for Mom to respect Dad. Even adult kids love this! Most of all, they have the incredible privilege of having parents who love God.

Begin today to treat your husband in a kind, generous manner. You don't need to make any announcements or proclamations…just do it! He may be suspicious at first, but we doubt he'll complain. Deep within he'll be pleased, and more than that, God will be pleased. As you begin living this way, you'll discover that there's no better feeling than knowing that your life is pleasing to God.

Is your marriage in need of a fresh start?
Why not let the fresh start begin with you—today!

From Rejected to Dearly Loved

Who Better to Resurrect an Ash Heap of a Marriage
than the Creator of Marriage Himself?

MARLA KLOECKNER

otive is an interesting thing. In a sense, our motives define us as little else does. For example, some go to church to worship God; others go because it looks good. One friend went because it gave her an opportunity to wear the beautiful clothes her mother made for her!

Motive is especially interesting when it comes to marriage. Wes and I (Connie) often talk with our three teenage daughters about not only what to look for in a mate, but also the whys of this decision. Marriage is challenging enough when the motives are pure and honorable. But when they're something other than that— such as marrying a beautiful and kind woman because it makes you look good—it becomes a slippery slope indeed. When a woman discovers that she is simply a token corporate wife, something is bound to happen.

There were times years ago when family and friends likened my marriage to a Barbie and Ken matchup. While my husband could pass for Ken, my thought each morning when I gazed into that unfriendly mirror was, *Thank goodness for Revlon!*

Is there such a thing as a perfect storybook marriage? I thought there was, and I felt I was living it! I loved my husband, Dale, and he treated me royally. I would do anything for him. And with our positive personalities and kind demeanors, it seemed easy to keep our dream matchup alive.

Dale and I met on a blind date. If love at first sight exists, we experienced it. He was a handsome gentleman with a great sense of humor. To top it off, we belonged to the same denomination of church. What more could a girl want? Within two years we married—even though Vietnam loomed heavily over us and Dale's birth date was number one in the draft. We began our new life together in San Francisco, where he was stationed with the army.

On the first weekend following our wedding, I discovered that Dale was unwilling to attend church with me. He said he had gone before only out of courtesy to his folks! The first weekend in our tiny apartment I remember thinking, *Oh, Lord, have I made a mistake?* Unfortunately, marriage counseling was almost unheard of back then.

Still, we sailed along, enjoying our simple life. When we hit bumps, I discovered it was much easier to steady the boat by going along with my husband. Church was the first item to be cast overboard. We avoided confrontation and life was great. I was steering the ship at home, which was fine with him.

After Dale's time in the army came a new job and two children. We both agreed it would be good for the kids to attend Sunday school and church. However, this didn't mean Dale would participate if he had better things to do—like playing golf. He seemed pleased with the situation. He was steadily climbing the company ladder while I was raising our two boys. A quiet lull set in—but I failed to realize that I was on a slowly leaking boat.

Then one day, Dale stunned me with the news that he had married me because I was nice and because it was expected of him. I realized we were in trouble—Ken and Barbie's ship was quickly taking on water.

My life came to a screeching halt. To be told that you were never really loved is devastating. Barbie hadn't been living the dream life at all—she was merely a token corporate wife! Time seemed to stand still as this news sunk in. I was experiencing a fatal blow to everything I had trusted and on which so much of my life was centered. I had just witnessed the death of my marriage and was in disbelief. Little did I know, this realization was the beginning of what was to become the most defining and blessed time of my life.

Finally, God had my full attention.

Dale and I limped along, trying to salvage the remaining pieces of our marriage for the sake of our children and his professional future. Plus, I remembered my vows before God—for better *and* worse. Well, the worse was here! I fell to my knees one morning while making the bed and cried out to God, *I need Your help!* A minute later I turned on the radio to find some soothing music, when I heard something about

God and His love. I dusted off my Bible and started reading living words that began to give me hope. Why had I ignored God all these years? What did He want me to do with this sham of a marriage? He began to gently answer my questions and teach me, even through my deep depression.

Though in my eyes I didn't have a real husband, the Lord showed me that as a rejected wife with a distressed spirit, *He* was my husband and I needed to listen to Him.[2] My life, mind, and heart needed to be renewed and transformed.[3] I clung to the verses He showed me until He made them my nature. Finally it dawned on me that His desire was to *change me* into a new woman—one that He could use for His purposes. The question was this: Would I become His student? My answer: Without doubt! I would be a Mary at His feet every moment, if He would have me. And of course He would!

The things the Lord taught me are endless. But a significant lesson that comes to mind is the truth about forgiveness. With His help, I could forgive anyone. I learned that I was just as much a sinner as my husband or anyone else, and that *my sin* had nailed Him to the cross. I began to pray regularly, and as my love for God grew, I found that I could love my husband in a new way. Dale, however, became more frustrated with me and our struggle intensified. He couldn't understand the peace I had or my newfound relationship with Christ.

I sought Christian guidance, but the best counsel I found was in His Word. I remembered a Bible study a friend had invited me to, which is where I was challenged to apply God's Word to my life. I prayed for Dale's salvation daily. I was committed to praying for this as long as it took—even if it took years or happened on his deathbed. But God softened my husband's heart long before I expected. Several years ago, Dale committed his life to Christ.

From the ash heap of our marriage, the Lord has miraculously brought forth restoration and resurrection! Our marriage, once dead, is now alive. It is founded on the Rock. We are both serving the Lord in various ministries, and our love for each other has been renewed and runs deeper and stronger than ever before. What a joy it is to tell others that I am married to a new man! They think it is a second marriage and a second man—and in a way it is. No more dreams of Ken and Barbie. This marriage is for real and better than that dream ever was.

Marla and Dale are very special to me (Nancy). Marla is one of those women who simply glows. She is full of joy and fun to be with and teaches a widely attended Bible study. Because of Dale's influence in my son's life, Paul is now active in a ministry to children. Marla and Dale have become fruitful Christians that the Lord is using to encourage other couples who are struggling.

Isn't it encouraging to know that the Lord can take the ash heaps of our lives and use them as a pulpit for His glory?

Have you surrendered your ash heaps to God?

"I Never Knew That!"

What You Don't Know Can Hurt You

CINDY GENSLER

We teach a class on how to be a wife. We call it simply the Wife Class. It's so interesting to watch the faces of the various women in the class as the weeks go by. One of the most memorable is Cindy. As we taught, we noticed that Cindy's facial expressions could hold their own against any Oscar-winning actress. But Cindy wasn't acting. Her expressions were for real and mirrored what was going on in her heart.

For example, we might tell the class that after her relationship with God, the primary role of ministry for a woman is her husband…only to be met by a stunned expression, complete with furrowed brow and wide eyes. An audible gasp was thrown in on occasion.

If we asked the piercing question "Is your husband lonely?"⁴ Cindy might look around the room to see if anyone else was struggling with this strange concept. She had no idea that as a wife, she was called to be an "aloneness fighter" in her marriage. And she wasn't sure she liked the calling, either!

But the day came, and surely all of heaven rejoiced, when this precious wandering sheep began to understand that these words *were from the Shepherd's own pen, written directly for her. Not only did she get it; she practiced it. And wonder of wonders, she later took this very teaching to her own church, blessing countless women with the same wonderful news that freed her to love her husband in a new way.*

Could your love for your husband use some freshening up? Then you're going to love Cindy's story. As Cindy says, "If I can get it, anyone can!"

For thirteen years of my marriage, I lived in the dark about what my role as a wife truly was. I had absolutely no idea that I was called to be a helper and completer.[5] So of course I wasn't!

My gratitude for my role as a wife began the minute the Holy Spirit opened my eyes to the truth about this vital role, and I have never been the same since.

With the godly advice of some older women and a heart made willing by God, the revamping in my life began. For the next three years, the Lord transformed my heart and mind to line up with His will. I learned that after my relationship with Jesus, my relationship with my husband is to be my first priority. I never knew that! Imagine having a job for years and never knowing what your job description was!

I discovered that Greg's leadership is God's best for me and that it's a covering of protection for me. Allowing your husband to lead brings a woman such freedom—yet is so opposite of what the world says. No wonder women get confused. I relinquished the desire to control the overall picture of our household and gave it to Greg. This meant the responsibility of leading our home and family fell to him, where it should be. I still give input, of course, but I trust Greg to do what is best—and trust God to lead him.

Greg and I are blessed with two sons, and I'm thankful for the opportunity to model by the Spirit's power how a wife should conduct herself. It's sobering for a mother to realize that who her sons one day marry will be determined to a certain degree by how they see her. I want my boys to have a mom who honors God in her marriage and in her life. When you do the right thing before God, it impacts so many lives—even generations—beyond what we can ever know.

At times, I felt hopeless in my marriage and wondered if a different spouse would make my life easier. At times, I felt I deserved better. At times, I wondered if changing my approach to marriage was actually worth it. These thoughts are lies from the enemy that must be squashed. Renewing my mind daily gives me the perspective I need to be victorious.

I no longer feel responsible for how Greg lives his life or the choices he makes. And one of the beautiful results is that as I've entrusted Greg to God, He has led Greg in wisdom and truth. I'm responsible for my choices though, so I strive to be the woman God wants me to be. I want to please God, and I pray that He will equip me with the incorruptible beauty of a gentle and quiet spirit, which is very precious in His sight.[6]

For years I was focused on myself, so I know firsthand how easily a person can drift away from God when that happens. A self-centered life is not precious or pleasing to God in any way. I now know the joy that comes from being focused *on God* and living to please Him. I still stumble, but when I do, I ask His forgiveness and keep going forward.

Greg and I have been married for seventeen years now—all glory to God! He continues to transform us and is so faithful. I look forward to what lies ahead—it's an adventure, and the best is yet to come.

What Cindy shares is profound! You can be a self-centered wife or you can be a God-centered wife—but you can't be both! And, oh, the blessings that come when you ask God to help you be a wife His way.

What Cindy said about her boys is especially noteworthy. If you have sons, think about this: Would you want them to marry a woman who treats them in the same manner you treat your husband? If you have daughters, would you want them to treat their husbands the way they see you treating their dad? If not, why not become a wife and mother who models for her kids what it looks like to please God? Perhaps you think it's too late—but it's never too late. My (Nancy) children were teenage and older before I even owned my first Bible, yet recently my daughter called and said, "Mom, would you teach me how to be a godly wife?" My heart was overjoyed.

With God, there's no such thing as a late start! He's ready to help you begin right where you are…just as you are. And when He's the Instructor, you'll be able to say with Cindy, "The best thing I ever did for my marriage was to do it His way!"

Are you living—and being a wife—His way?

Politically Incorrect

What Seems Superficial to a Woman May Be Core to a Man

ANONYMOUS

*A*ll of us have to eat humble pie from time to time. One of the many times I (Connie) have was shortly after the births of our twin daughters. Before the girls were born, I felt there was absolutely no reason any child should be allowed to whine. A good mother should be able to nip it in the bud!

You can imagine what happened. Our daughters redefined whining! No matter what I tried, they whined. They never slept—they were too busy whining. To top things off, Wes's job often meant he worked twelve to fourteen hours a day, six, sometimes seven days a week. He'd come home exhausted, only to be met at the door by a weary wife and two unhappy babies. Life was a zoo!

I'll never forget the day he walked in the door and thanked me for putting on lipstick. I hadn't worn lipstick for months—who had time to know where the lipstick was, let alone actually put it on! But that day I had smeared some on just before he got home.

This poor man is reduced to thanking me for wearing lipstick, I thought. I was in the trenches and my external appearance showed it. My typical uniform was a comfortable, baggy sweat suit or a worn-out robe. I had taken casual to a whole new (sub)level

41

when the girls were babies. (To this day, elastic remains one of my favorite man-made products!) The days when I had dressed to look nice for him were long gone.

What I didn't know then was how important a woman's appearance is to her husband. It is of great interest to her hus-band—even when they have young children. A smart woman not only recognizes this, but does something about it!

Nancy and Connie recently released a book called *The Politically Incorrect Wife*. Perhaps my chapter should have gone in that book, because what I'm about to share is about as politically incorrect as it gets, especially coming from a woman.

Knowing that most women contributing to this book would share from a spiritual perspective, I decided to share from a decidedly different one. First let me say that, without question, the best thing I ever did for my marriage was to ask Jesus to be my Lord and Savior. In fact, this is the best thing I've ever done, period!

The second-best thing I ever did for my marriage—apart from the spiritual—was to lose weight. That's probably not what most of you want to read about, but I feel compelled to share because it's such a big deal for most men—far bigger than most women realize.

When my husband and I married, I was slender and attractive. However, after the birth of our first baby, I retained some "baby weight." Three babies later, I was forty pounds heavier than I'd been on our wedding day. I knew this bothered my husband. He even attempted to share his thoughts with me. But I was hurt when he did and would make him feel guilty for not loving me the way I was, extra pounds and all.

He ended up looking shallow, which was as I felt it

should be. I was raising our kids, keeping the home in order, and doing a host of other things, and all he seemed to care about was my physical appearance. I felt he needed to grow up and get his priorities straight. We lived in this pattern for years. Over time we drifted apart emotionally, and our sexual life suffered as well. I had no desire to make love to such a shallow man whose love was so conditional.

Then one day a friend gave me Patrick Morley's book *What Husbands Wish Their Wives Knew About Men*. In the chapter "Appearance: Why a Man Wants His Wife to Look Good," Mr. Morley writes:

> What first attracted him to his wife was her looks, and they are still important to him.... If I picked up anything during the research for this book it is that husbands want to stay married. They also want you to continue "attracting" them.... If any wife reading this book could say, "If my husband died, after my mourning time I would lose thirty pounds, fix my hair a new way, and buy a new wardrobe," she can be almost certain of this: Her husband secretly wishes she would go ahead and do it now. Here's the point: Men don't stop caring about "attraction."[7]

He then goes on to describe the very pattern my husband and I had lived in for years. He says that if a woman ignores the issue or becomes so upset that she doesn't deal with it constructively, she risks a downward spiral in the marriage:

> First, the wife lets her appearance slip (assuming he does not). Her husband attempts to talk to her about it. It becomes a sore spot. He stops bringing it up.

I believe after a few rejected attempts at communication on this, a husband will no longer be able to muster the courage to tell his wife exactly how he feels about her appearance if she will not (1) make him the primary audience for her appearance and (2) work at remaining as physically attractive as she was when they married, reasonably proportioned to the years gone by.

Though he stops bringing it up, the issue hasn't gone away. He later stops saying nice things about her appearance. His romantic interest wanes. Her emotional bank account goes empty. An emotional distance develops between them. They coexist.

Be willing to "hear" your husband.... If you sense from your husband a lack of romantic interest, looks, and physical touch, consider your appearance.

Be willing to make appropriate changes.[8]

I began to realize that it wasn't my husband's shallowness that made him want me to be attractive; it's simply the way he thinks as a man. Men are visual; women aren't. Women long to be cherished; men don't as much. This doesn't mean we're right and they're wrong, does it? Of course not! Then shouldn't the same be true in reverse—that maybe it isn't wrong for a guy to want his wife to look nice?

After twenty-five years of marriage, I've come to believe this truth: God placed in every woman's heart the desire to be loved. That's inherent to us. I also believe that He placed in every man's heart the desire to be respected, as well as the desire to have a spouse who makes an effort to stay attractive. This is inherent to men. It doesn't mean they're shallow, or louts, or wrong. It's simply part of their make-up.

So I began exercising and watching what I ate. (I was amazed at how much I ate! I always thought I ate very little—probably because I grazed my way through the day and didn't eat much at mealtimes.) Over a period of months, I lost several pounds and have managed to keep them off. My husband is thrilled. He never stopped loving me before, but as he says, "It's just so much easier to feel love for you now." Our relationship is warmer than it has ever been—in every area.

I must admit, though, that some days I still get irritated about this. I find myself wishing that my weight wasn't such a big deal to him. But it is. Just like feeling loved and cherished is a big deal to me. He doesn't try to talk me out of feeling that, so why do I sometimes feel so self-righteous in thinking his wants are wrong? It can become a vicious cycle if you're not careful.

I know that many women feel justified in this matter—believing it's his problem, not theirs. But to disregard this issue undermines your husband as a man. Blaming your husband for the way he was created carries grave consequences.

Someone once said that there will be no scales in heaven. I say, "*Hallelujah!*" But until I get there, I'm committed to showing my love for my husband in the way I look—both inside *and* outside.

Looks matter to a man. That's just the way it is! A pastor once addressed this topic in a sermon: "Sometimes my wife gets up on Saturday mornings and, knowing we're going to be working in the yard, doesn't do a lot with herself. She'll throw on some shorts and a T-shirt and off we'll go. Other times, we might be headed to a meeting, and she'll spend a little more time in front of the mirror, making certain she looks nice. I must admit, I prefer those mornings she spends a little more time in front of the mirror!"

Politically incorrect? Who's to say!

Of course, a woman shouldn't have to "earn" her husband's love by what she weighs, and too often this is the message many husbands send. God's Word commands a man to love his wife. It even gets specific—"as Christ loved the church."⁹ For a man to imply to his wife that her worth is directly proportional to her weight is wrong. A day will come when these men will have to give an account of their behavior before God Himself. Undoubtedly they'll wish they had behaved differently.

So although a woman's external appearance matters greatly to most husbands, it's not to be what defines her. More important than this by far is the hidden person of her heart—her inner beauty.

It's a fortunate man whose wife attends to both her inner and her outer beauty. Surely when a woman does this, her husband is pleased. And surely God is, too.

Do you make it a priority to look nice for your husband?
Do you hold against him his desire
for you to continue to be attractive?

Anything You Can Do I Can Do Better!

That age-old battle for control can rear its ugly head at any moment, especially in marriage. No matter the issue, the women whose stories you're about to read once felt their ways were superior to their husbands'.
Far superior, in fact! Little did they realize that this mindset was a stumbling block to happiness not only in their marriages, but also in their own lives.

Bring Down That Wall!

Walls Are Good for Holding Up Houses,
but Not for Holding Together Relationships

CYNTHIA HEALD

One of the most moving speeches we've ever heard was given by President Ronald Reagan. He was standing in front of the wall that had divided East and West Germany for many years. As he concluded, his voice thundered with passion and he issued this challenge: "Mr. Gorbachev, bring down this wall!" Not long after that message, the wall came down. It was a great historical moment, captured forever on film and in the hearts of all who saw it.

Some walls are invisible, but they can be just as divisive. The worst is a wall that is silently put in place by a wife or husband because of unmet expectations. This wall can be nearly impossible to bring down—unless, of course, God steps in.

With a deep sigh, I reluctantly prayed, *Okay, Lord, I give Jack to You.* I was offering up this prayer in response to God's prompting in my heart. It was clear that He was asking me to release my husband into His hands.

The year was 1972. Jack was a busy veterinarian who

typically worked fourteen to sixteen hours a day. He had hired additional help, but his schedule had changed only a little. We had four young children, and with an absentee husband and father, I was beginning to feel sorry for myself. Jack was rarely home for dinner and was frequently called out early in the morning. Whenever we planned to have time to ourselves, it was more often than not interrupted by a cow having a calf!

Our social activities were always tentative. Most of the time I attended dinners and functions by myself. It was hard to schedule any time to entertain people in our home because there was always the possibility of an emergency. I remember one night we had invited three couples over for dinner. Jack felt certain he could be there. I decided to make the evening special by using our china and silver, and I had fun preparing something besides Cheerios, applesauce, and little bites of chicken. As our guests arrived at six-thirty, Jack called from a ranch saying that he needed to suture a horse that had a deep cut. He arrived at nine, all bloody and tired, just in time for coffee.

My standard responses were impatience and frustration. Something had to be done! I had to make Jack see that he must make some changes. My first tactic was to become a martyr. I sighed, whined, drooped my shoulders. "It's not fair that I bear the burden of raising our children and tending to our home. It's not right that I never know when you'll be here." Jack would listen. He, too, would sigh and droop his shoulders and agree that it was not the best arrangement…but nothing changed. So my complaining got a little louder and harsher. All my dear husband could do was say that it hurt him that I was unhappy but that he had done all he could to be available to us. He reminded me that he took the children with him as much as possible, had an answering service to screen calls, and had hired help. What else could he do?

Resigned, I thought, *Okay. I'll just be in charge of our children, our home, and even Jack.* Instead of trying to adapt to my husband's schedule, I took control of our lives. If he fit in with our plans, good; if not, he was the one missing out. The problem with this approach was that it put a wall between Jack and me. I essentially withdrew from him emotionally. But after a few weeks, I felt more alone than ever. I loved my husband and wanted togetherness. What could I do?

It was at this time that I began to hear the Lord's promptings in my heart: "Cynthia, can you set your husband free from your control? Can you learn to be content in these circumstances? Do you believe that My grace is sufficient for your life? Can you take delight in doing My will instead of your own?"

I don't know, Lord. I'm afraid that if I give up control, nothing will change.

"Cynthia, even if your situation never changes, am I enough for you? Can you trust Me to be all that you need? My child, I want you to understand that being a godly wife has nothing to do with your husband's actions, but everything to do with how much you love Me and desire to do My will. You bring Me glory by your surrender and trust in My plans for you."

Thank You, Father. I do give Jack to You. He is Yours...and I am Yours. I place our lives into Your hands.

It was the best thing I ever did for my marriage—that day I surrendered not only my penchant to control, but also myself and my marriage to the only One who controls all things.

Not only did Cynthia give her husband to God; she surrendered herself to Him as well. It's only from this position that God will work out His great purpose for a person's life. Women worldwide have been blessed by Cynthia's writing. She is a bestselling author and a gifted speaker. During a women's retreat she led, I (Nancy) first sensed God calling me to serve Him in our church. How thankful I am that Cynthia listened to God and acted on what He told her to do—it brought down the wall that isolated her not only from her husband, but also from a thriving relationship with Jesus Himself.

Is there a wall in your marriage?
Is there a wall in your relationship with God?
Ask God to help you "bring down that wall!"

The Stainless Steel Coffee Mug

A Pot of Coffee Made with Love Can
Warm a Person More than You Might Think

DIANE JELKIN

It seems that every great change begins small. In this story, from a small thought came a small purchase, which led to a small act of service. A small change of heart began in the giver, then in the receiver. An old adage says that if you keep doing the same thing, you'll keep getting the same results. In Diane's case, she became weary of her way of doing things and wanted to make a change. It's guaranteed: When you make a change, something will happen. The cycle you've been in will be broken, and frequently the principle of sowing and reaping will come into play.[10] Often the recipient of your kindness will respond with kindness, but even if he doesn't notice, don't worry—God notices and says, "When you do good, expecting nothing in return, your reward will be great."[11] Your reward will come from God Himself!

❧

Who would've thought that buying my husband a stainless steel travel mug would be one of the best things I ever did for my marriage? Let me explain.

Several years ago, I reached a point where I was tired of being unhappy in my marriage. Someone needed to make some changes, and it wasn't my husband (I had already tried that prayer!).

I knew I needed help—I just didn't know where to begin. But God, in His wonderful mercy, led me to just the right Bible study, and I began to see that I was not the wife God called me to be or that my husband deserved. I hadn't made Mel a priority in my life. My words and actions were not always kind or respectful—to say the least.

One day I finally got the message. God got through to me. He was calling me to be obedient to Him: "Show Mel you love him, Diane. Don't be afraid. Trust Me. I'll show you the way."

About that time, a godly friend told me that every morning she takes coffee to her husband in bed. What a commitment. Every day! *Every single day.* My mind immediately began to resist: *What if I'm mad or irritated and don't feel like making his coffee? Then what?* Besides, Mel left too early in the morning for me to do that.

But God reminded me of something Mel had said just a few days earlier: He stops at a gas station for coffee every morning, which is why he leaves so early. By the time he drives there, goes in, fixes his coffee, chats with the attendant, and heads back out, he's in the thick of rush hour.

That's when the idea hit me: Buy him a travel mug, get the coffee ready the night before, and set the automatic timer.

What a great idea, Lord! (And I truly believe this idea was from Him; it certainly wasn't mine.) When I told Mel that his coffee would be ready the next morning, it was as if he'd just played his best round of golf. He was ecstatic!

After a few weeks of this routine, I noticed that Mel started spending time with God before he left for work. He later told me that not having to stop for coffee gave him extra time, and he'd decided to use it to read his Bible or study a devotional.

In the process my attitude toward Mel began to change dramatically. It felt good to do something for him. While making the coffee, I would pray for him. During the day, I would glance over at the coffee pot, think of him, and realize just how blessed I was to have him for my husband. My love for him blossomed, and we began enjoying one another like we hadn't in years. Mel has since joined a men's Bible study. He is growing spiritually and really sensing God's presence in his life.

Yes, there are times when I'm irritated with him and don't feel like making his coffee. When I feel this way, God reminds me that I'm actually serving *Him* when I serve my husband. A simple stainless steel travel mug will always be a reminder to me that God can use even the smallest things to bring restoration to a marriage and glory to Him.

Don't you love Diane's honesty? Even though she doesn't always feel like making Mel's coffee, she does it anyway! Preparing your husband a cup of coffee is about so much more than just coffee—it gives a glimpse into your heart, and, as in this case, can have a huge impact on a husband's spiritual life. Who would think that a cup of coffee could result in his spending more time with God? Undoubtedly, Mel's entire day—his interactions with others, his performance at work—was filtered through knowing his wife cared about him deeply.

Diane is one of my (Connie) closest friends and I treasure her friendship greatly. She was one of the first people to encourage me to consider writing. Everyone who spends even a moment with her comes away feeling accepted and loved, which I believe happens because she goes to the Source that never runs dry for her own love and encouragement—and gets filled to overflowing by the Maker Himself.

What one kindness are you willing to do for your husband every single day?

"I Nominate Myself Leader of the Home!"

Giving up the Reins of a Horse Is Far Easier than Giving up Reign of the Home

NENA BUCKLEY

A friend of ours recently told us about a time her husband came home from work, his arms laden with gifts. It was Boss's Day, and the gifts were from the people he supervised.

He jokingly told his wife that he'd thought about stopping by the florist's on the way home to buy her a bouquet because she was the boss at their house. She vehemently disagreed, assuring him that he was the leader. Their young child, though, sided with Dad. "Everyone knows you're the real boss, Mom."

She told us it was as if a knife had been twisted in her heart. What am I doing? she thought. She knew her child was right. And she vowed to change.

Since the beginning of time, women have wrestled with the desire to usurp their husbands' rightful place as leader in the home. When a woman does this, she's undermining the very foundation of marriage that God set in place for her.

Why live on a wobbly foundation when you can live on a

strong, steady one? Even if your husband isn't a natural-born leader, he may surprise you with the strides he'll make if you just get out of the way and allow him to lead!

I had the incredible experience of leading my husband to Jesus when we were dating. He said that my beliefs made so much sense to him, and he immediately became a believer.

I felt that I was the mature one in our marriage and needed to share all my wisdom and experience with my husband—who I saw as just a "babe" in Christ. Christians can so be haughty; spiritual pride can set in without your even recognizing it.

And that's what happened with me. I believed that I was stronger in my faith and understood God's plan better than my husband did. When it came to church involvement, I felt I knew what it took and could serve more effectively in various positions. I was asked to serve on the board at our church and thought this was just as it should be. Remember, I was the "mature" one. Similar situations happened frequently, and each time I was more than happy to take my "rightful" position.

But God knew that this wasn't the correct order of things. In His gracious mercy, He took us away from the church we had become so involved in to give me some time to see my weakness. We moved to a small town, where I felt alone and unneeded. Slowly I began to realize that I was dominating our marriage—and even liking it. But I kept hearing God say, "Let go."

It took a year for the changes to take place, but in God's timing we moved back to our former church. But this time was different: I stayed in the background and supported my husband, who was soon asked to serve on the board. He was outstanding in this ministry. I know God used that time away to mature both of us—my husband's leadership skills and my willingness to let go.

I learned that when I let God have His way, the reward is great and God is honored. God showed me that the husband is to be the leader of the home. And as I have allowed my husband his rightful position, he has blossomed beyond belief. He has been an outstanding role model for our sons in how to lead a family. I shudder to think what might have happened if I hadn't changed my ways—they would have missed the blessing of knowing what it is to have their father as head of the home.

Men today need to take up their leadership roles, and we need to support them in this effort. My greatest joy is to see my husband do well and be a strong leader. I'm forever thankful that God showed me the error of my ways and gave me the grace to change.

His ways are so much better than mine!

Is a struggle for control going on in your home? There was in both of ours. For years, we fought our husbands for the leadership role. Both Ray and Wes learned that often it was easiest just to give in. And we were more than happy to let them!

Although we didn't know each other at the time, our lives were amazingly similar, both marked by constant frustration and a lack of peace.

Often, when a woman embraces God's plan for her as a wife, change begins. That's what happened for us. We sometimes wonder why we were so willing to live such churned-up lives—but you see, we just didn't know.

Maybe you didn't know before, either…or maybe you knew but didn't care! Don't let that be the case any longer. Let go of your "old ways," and see the myriad of blessings that will come as you embrace God's best for your life—and your family's life. You'll never want to go back.

Do you afford your husband his rightful place as the leader of your home?

The Dance

*Why Do We Love for Men to Lead When
We're Dancing but Not in Everyday Life?*

KAREN KOSSE

*H*ow romantic! *That's exactly what I thought when my
(Nancy) dad told me how he met my mother.*

She and Dad worked in the same department store in
Baltimore, Maryland, but had never spoken to one another. Both
happened to go to a dance one evening, each with another person,
but they exchanged glances. Dad decided to ask her to dance. And
as they danced, Mom kissed him! My sister and I were astonished
to hear that our very composed and proper mother would ever do
such a thing…but not nearly as dumbfounded as Dad was! She
immediately and permanently won his heart.

I remember taking dancing lessons with Ray, who will readily
admit to two left feet. He was the star of the class because his tech-
nique was, to put it politely, so unique! It was wildly funny to try to
follow his lead, and good sport that he was, even he had to laugh. It
was a different story in our marriage, though. I wanted to lead,
which was neither fun nor funny. For in marriage, God has ordained
that a wife is to be led by her husband. This kind of "dancing" is
absolutely beautiful and is applauded by an audience of One—the
One who created the dance.

Marriage was the furthest thing from my mind when Jim and I went on our first date. I just wanted to have a good time. And we did! We danced all night, and when I got home I wrote in my diary that he was the man I was going to marry. I was focusing on his great dancing skills and the fun we had together—not great reasons to pick a husband! But I also saw in him qualities that would make him a wonderful mate. I knew I would be well taken care of by him.

We had a fast and rocky courtship and were married ten months later. I didn't have a clue about how to be a wife. I knew I was supposed to cook the meals, clean the house, and have babies—so that's what I did. Ten years into our marriage, Jim's focus was on his career and making money and mine was on getting a bigger house, taking care of our three children, and getting involved in activities outside the home. I was functioning as a wife and mother, but was totally disillusioned because I had taken over the leadership in our home.

God knew this and set a plan in motion to help me become a godly wife. Feeling frustrated with our marriage, my husband and I were coaxed into attending a Marriage Encounter Weekend. Jim went reluctantly, expecting me to lower the boom on him, which was my intention! But God changed my heart with two huge revelations.

As we listened to the speakers, I realized first that God had never been welcomed into our marriage. He was an uninvited guest on our wedding day and had been sent home after the reception. I knew I needed to make Him central to our marriage. Second, I learned that love is a decision, not a feeling. I had never heard that before and realized I had never made that decision. Fortunately, Jim had made that choice from the beginning and had fought for us. That weekend I decided—for the first time—to love my husband and give up the role of leader. Much to my surprise, I found that with each change I loved him more! And I discovered that deciding to love him isn't a one-time thing. I have to decide to love him even when I don't *feel* love for him.

It has been amazing to see the correlation between my relationship with God and my relationship with my husband. God is no longer an uninvited guest in our marriage. He is an integral part of our relationship, and that has sweetened everything.

Jesus accepts wedding invitations! That reality dawned on Karen in a fresh and personal way. Remember when Jesus attended the wedding at Cana? The wine had run out, so He instructed the servants to put water in the water pots. After they did this, they tasted it and discovered it was better than the wine they had been serving.

Karen had become disillusioned with her marriage and had run out of love for her husband. When she realized that Jesus had been an uninvited guest at their wedding, she set things right. She invited Him into her marriage and gave Him the central position. When that happened, Jesus filled her "water pots"—He changed everything and made the love they had for each other sweeter than when they first married. And He can do the same for you!

Karen's aim is to be like Christ, and her daily prayer is, Lord, make me more like Jesus and lead us in our "dance."

May we all aim so high!

Do you need "dancing lessons"?

Yo-Yo Diets and Camels

A Wife Should Guard Her Husband's
Heart with All Her Might

Tiet Parsons

In a sermon, our pastor once referred to what a fabulous cook his wife is. "Sometimes," he said, "all I can do is murmur, 'Mmm, mmm, mmm.' It's that good."

On the way home from church, I (Connie) commented to Wes that I couldn't recall him ever saying "Mmm, mmm, mmm" about anything I'd cooked.

He paused for a moment. "No, I don't think I have."

We looked at each other and laughed. The truth is, I don't like to cook and when I do I often don't have all the ingredients I need, so my dish comes out tasting less than "Mmm."

That's kind of how marriage is, too. Unless you have all the ingredients, the results are going to be far from delicious!

I met John in 1975, at a refugee camp at Ft. Chaffee, Arkansas. I was a Vietnamese refugee and he was an English teacher. After I left the camp, we continued to stay in touch through letters and phone calls, and as a result of our communication,

John brought me to the Lord. We married two years after we met. Strangely enough, the cultural and language differences were not the source of our marital struggles; the personality differences were!

My husband is patient and easygoing, while I have a temper and am analytical and critical. I often describe myself as someone who has a perfectionist's eye without the perfectionist's ability to achieve perfection.

For the first several years of our marriage, I studied the Bible only sporadically. To me, it was like reading a book on constitutional law—it supplied a lot of interesting information, but was difficult to absorb and retain. I had learned how to pray, but I didn't incorporate it into my daily life. Even worse, I didn't know anything about the wife's role in marriage, particularly regarding submission. Besides, I thought that when I came to America, I shed the expectations of an Eastern culture, in which a wife's fate lay at her husband's mercy. Whoever heard of a submissive wife in America? I thought submission was an antiquated concept that had been abolished long ago.

Looking back, I can see that I was such a spoiled spouse, but at the time I didn't think so! My picture of a selfish wife was a woman who decked herself out in expensive clothes and fine jewelry and expected her husband to cater to her every whim. She sulked, nagged, or threw fits when her desires weren't met.

That last part sometimes got me wondering.... But I didn't sulk, only kept silent. I definitely didn't nag; I just liked to make sure he remembered. As for throwing fits, even my mother-in-law laughingly, yet wholeheartedly, agreed that she and I did not get angry unless we were provoked!

I felt that my way was better than John's in almost every

area. The way he loaded the dishwasher was different (and wrong), and I even shrieked at the way he changed the baby's diaper. And I thought I wasn't spoiled!

My dissatisfaction with John progressed to the point that I blamed him for *my* shortcomings. His complete acceptance of me, however, put the burden of change where it needed to be—on me. Self-discipline was not my cup of Starbucks coffee. I needed someone to straighten me out, which sent me down another bunny trail: Oh, how I wished my husband were strong enough to change me! But he couldn't win—I saw everything he did as a failure.

When children entered into the picture, I wanted to be in God's Word more so I could teach them about Him. I read Bible stories to them, helped them memorize Scripture, and taught them to pray. And strangely and miraculously, I began to grow in knowledge, too. I found that every time I came under God's teaching, I had more control over my sharp tongue and capricious emotions. My eyes were opened in many ways.

I read a powerful verse to my oldest child about one of Jesus' disciples: "Because you have seen me, you have believed; blessed are those who have not seen and yet have believed."[12] As I read it, I realized that this was not just empty information in a dead textbook—the realization sent chills up and down my spine.

Later, during a time of struggle, I read, "Her husband has full confidence in her."[13] I was so convicted of my ungodliness. I couldn't honestly say that my husband's heart was safe with me. How many times must he have wondered what he would face in the lioness's den when he got home from work? He had made many overtures during this time of personal struggle, yet I grudgingly picked and chose what was worth keeping. Of course I taught my children to receive graciously what others offered, but what I preached wasn't how I lived.

My problem was that I stayed in God's Word about as faithfully as a person on a yo-yo diet. When I was doing well, I would become overconfident and stray from the right path. Then I'd grow irritated, fault John, and blame God for not changing me for good. I would cry out miserably, *I want to be a godly wife. Why don't You make my path less bumpy and my husband less blemished?*

I once wondered dejectedly, *If God is so good, why do I feel so bad?* The answer popped into my head almost audibly: "Jesus felt worse, and did He complain? How about the apostle Paul? Stephen?" The list went on, to all the men and women of faith. Etched indelibly in my memory was the reminder that good feelings are not what He promises us, but rather the intrinsic joy that comes from being obedient to what is right in His eyes. I could not succeed in teaching my children to fully follow His Word and His ways if *I* resisted this truth.

The light finally came on, and I realized that I am not made like a camel, which needs to go to a water source for its fill only once every three months. I must actively read God's Word and constantly obey. When I do that, He always gives me a pair of glasses with His perfect prescription to help me see things His way. My new vision affects my heart, which now is continually filled with love and gratefulness for my husband.

Wes and I have known and loved the Parsons for ten years. Tiet is a tiny dynamo of energy and John is rock solid in every way. Tiet's testimony reminds us of how the Israelites wandered around in the desert for forty years on what should have been an eleven-day trip.

Tiet got out of the desert when she realized she wasn't a camel (now there's profound theological truth!). You're not a camel, either. Being in God's Word daily and doing what it says is the best plan for staying out of the desert and getting on with your marriage and your life.

Just as we can't eat food once a month and expect to be physically healthy, we can't just nibble on God's Word now and then and expect to be spiritually healthy. We need to be feasting on His Word daily. That's the ticket to victorious living!

Does your husband's heart trust in you?

Hands Off!

"I Love You the Way You Are;
I Wouldn't Want to Change You or Even Rearrange You."[14]

But on the Other Hand...

BEV PUGH

*W*e think people need to rethink the wedding vows. *Everyone's familiar with better, worse, richer, poorer, sickness, health. Those promises are still completely on target. It's the first part that needs to be focused on: "I take you..." What does that mean anyway? "I take you"? Would the dreamlike state of the wedding ceremony be penetrated if the pastor lingered over those three words? And would the bride and groom be paying a little closer attention if we really meant what we were saying?*

What would happen if the pastor paused and said, "What were you really thinking when you just said, 'I take you'?" What would the bride say if the pastor asked, "Do you take his personality, his quirks, his idiosyncrasies, his intellect, his abilities, his dreams, his disappointments, his struggles, and everything that makes him him? And will you, dear bride, let him remain himself?"

Well, Bev's pastor didn't ask her those questions! Someone Greater asked her, years after her vows, and her response is breathtakingly beautiful.

68

I think I've found the perfect wedding gift: a beautiful calligraphy plaque of the old Puritan formula for a good marriage: "Choose your love...love your choice." As the years of my own marriage increase (thirty-seven to date), I find myself resting ever more deeply in the wisdom of that truth. What a simple formula for peace. I know how much I love to be in the presence of someone who loves and accepts me for who I really am. Not only is the wisdom of that little adage a great gift for newlyweds; it is also teaching me how to gift my own husband day by day as we share life together.

Why is it that a woman marries her very favorite guy in the whole wide world, and then sets out to "fix" him? If only he were more of a spiritual leader or less bossy or more fun or less sloppy or more *GQ* or less self-centered or more this, less that, and on and on. *I'll improve just a little bit on what God made. Wouldn't it be better if he were more like I want him to be? A little more like me, a little less like him?* I thought.

Lord, I think we've got something here. It seems to me I could help You improve this project of Yours. In fact, that is no doubt the very reason You gave this man to me. I'll just become sort of a surrogate Holy Spirit for you, kind of pick up Your slack, if you know what I mean, and get things moving in a better direction.

You see, I married a man of personal stability, quiet strength, focused purpose, and deep responsibility. He married a woman of great commitment and loyalty with fluctuating emotions, multiple focuses, and an unrecognized need for control. It has taken me years to understand the significance of our differences and the pure joy of letting God *use* those contrasts to hone both of us.

At some point in my marriage journey, I came across a

quote from Ruth Graham, that it was her job to "make Billy happy" and God's job to "make Billy holy." Well, that was news to me. So I took that concept thoughtfully before the Lord and gradually began to release back into His hands my agenda to reform my husband. I began by intentionally calling to mind the qualities that had so drawn me to him in the first place. I was humbled when I realized they were the very same qualities that were now driving me to become his "re-maker."

Gradually I saw that I had been replacing adjectives. *Stable* had become *stodgy*; *quiet* had deteriorated into *boring*; *focused* I now perceived as *stubborn*; *responsible* had descended into *predictable*. All in my own mind. My man hadn't changed, but the way I saw him had. I had lost the wonder of his God-given uniqueness.

God says that each of us is a creative masterpiece, a one-copy-only work of art directly from the hands of the Master Creator.[15] How arrogant of me to think that I could *or should* tamper with His masterpiece, my husband, the one He gave me to love and bless.

So I began to practice acceptance. I began to *look* for ways in which my husband's strengths could balance my weaknesses. I *chose* to recognize how his personality enriched our family. And I *learned* to focus on the many areas of my own little "work of art" that were badly in need of God's finishing touches. Needless to say, that became a full-time job in itself. I *admitted* that I was able to make changes only in me and was totally unable (and unauthorized!) to make changes in anyone else. I could leave the refining of the masterpiece in the hands of the One who designed him—and keep my hands off! What a gift of freedom that became both to my husband and me. Left to be himself, without criticism and pressure from me, my husband was free to flourish. His growth and refining became a matter between him and his Lord. I was freed to be his encourager, not his reformer.

> Oh, the comfort—
> the inexpressible comfort of feeling *safe* with a person—
> having neither to weigh thoughts nor measure words,
> but pouring them all right out,
> just as they are,
> chaff and grain together;
> certain that a faithful hand will take and sift them,
> keep what is worth keeping,
> and then with the breath of kindness blow the rest away.[16]

This is the kind of gift I want to give my dear husband. I have been deeply blessed that he has returned that same gift to me. But even without the return gifting, the freedom to let a person be himself is never given in vain. It is a gift pleasing to God because it reflects His way of relating to us. "Who are you to judge the servant of another? To his own master he stands or falls…we will all stand before the judgment seat of God. Therefore let us not judge one another *anymore,* but rather *determine* this—not to put an obstacle or a stumbling block in a brother's way."[17]

I can do that. I can bless my husband for who he is. I can rejoice in the blending and refining of our differences. I can get out of God's way and stop trying to do *His* job. I can—and will—keep my hands off God's masterpiece.

Can you imagine Al's freedom to love Bev? Think of what it means to be blessed simply for who you are! Bev may not have had to explain during her wedding ceremony what she meant by the words "I take you," but in the Lord's own special school for wives (called everyday life), she learned one of the most valuable truths of a successful marriage: Accept your husband as he is and allow God to do His work of transformation. When a wife does that, she will discover that the one who needs more "work" is herself!

Are you in the habit of saying to God,
"What You have made, I'll make better"?

Different Strokes for Different Folks

Ah, the Sweet Language of Love!

TERRY WALTERS

ave you ever traveled to a foreign country and not been able to understand a single thing being said? You spend more energy than ever trying to communicate, but to no avail.

Sometimes marriage can be like that. Men throw their hands up in frustration when their wives say they don't feel loved. What's a man supposed to do? he wonders. His wife is frustrated as well. Why doesn't he get it? she asks. It's so simple.

Learning to speak your husband's native tongue when it comes to love will mean the world to him. And when he reciprocates by learning yours, the delight is doubled.

As a young girl, I remember reading a book called *My Father Can Fix Anything*. I really thought it was written about my dad, because there was nothing he couldn't repair. When I got married, I assumed my husband would do this as well. Not only that, I also expected him to take care of my every emotional need. Poor guy—he was doomed to fail from the start!

What my dad did best was to make me feel really special. Steve and I had been married for ten years when I realized that this feeling was missing in our relationship. I remember sitting at the table and telling Steve I didn't think he loved me anymore. We talked about it a lot. The conversation always went something like this:

I'd say, "I don't think you love me anymore."

He'd respond with, "Yes, I do. What more can I do? I'm doing all I know how!"

I'd reply, "I can't believe you don't understand what I'm saying!"

We ran into this brick wall constantly but had no idea what to do about it. Thankfully we came across a wonderful book called *The Five Love Languages,* which helped us identify our problem and revolutionized our marriage. Dr. Gary Chapman explains that every person tends to give and receive love in one of five ways:

- Quality time
- Words of affirmation
- Gifts
- Acts of service
- Physical touch[18]

Each of us is born with something called a love tank. When we feel loved and secure, we're operating on a full love tank. But when it's empty, we no longer feel loved or cherished. You keep another person's love tank full only when you learn to speak his or her love language. That would explain why I didn't feel loved—I was operating on an empty tank.

My love language is "quality time," while Steve's is "acts of service." He has always been very helpful—but that didn't clearly speak love to me. What I needed was for him to spend time with me—quality time. This explains why I felt so loved by my dad. He took time for me and gave me his focused attention, which filled my tank.

As Steve began to understand this, he started calling me during the day just to let me know he was thinking of me. Next we started having "tea time"—even though we didn't always have tea. Usually we'd sit and talk after supper. The kids weren't allowed to interrupt unless they were bleeding or the house was on fire! It lasted only fifteen to twenty minutes, but it made me feel treasured. We also began having regular date nights.

For my part, I looked for ways to show love to Steve by doing acts of service for him. My role is easier because women typically do acts of service whether it's their love language or not—like preparing meals, doing laundry, etc. But I try to go beyond the usual so he feels especially loved.

Discovering and respecting each other's love language revolutionized our marriage. Although we occasionally still hit that brick wall, it's no longer the norm. What a relief! Who would've thought that the very area that once caused such frustration is now the reason for so much joy!

Terry is a close friend of ours and is married to a pastor. We especially admire how both she and Steve not only learned new information, but also actually put it into practice. This brings to mind some poignant words of Chuck Swindoll:

> *Let me mention one more "cheap substitute" so common among Christian wives in our day. It is learning about*

what's right rather than doing what is right.... Learning more truth is a poor and cheap substitute for stopping and putting into action the truth already learned.[19]

What a sweet fragrance it must be to the Lord when a woman puts into practice what He's revealing to her. Life is too short and relationships are too precious to be filled with "cheap substitutes."

Is your "wife life" filled with treasure,

or with cheap substitutes?

That's the Funniest Thing I Ever Heard! *Me* Change?

Tired of "just getting by" in your marriage?
Tired of mediocrity?
Tired of feeling frustrated, discouraged, and resigned?
So often, the turning point in a marriage is just a tiny
decision away. When a woman stops focusing on her
husband's "need" to change and chooses instead to
change herself, she'll be amazed at the results.

The Mother-in-Law

*Sometimes the Best Picture a Woman Has of Herself
Is How She Treats Those Closest to Her Husband*

DIANE REILLY
MARRIAGE MINISTRIES INTERNATIONAL

*A*lthough it happened over twenty years ago, I (Connie) remember it clearly. It was a Friday night, and Wes and I were headed out of Oklahoma City to visit our families for the weekend. Wes was still in school and I was working as an occupational therapist. We were so looking forward to this weekend away. To top it off, a favorite cousin of mine was getting married and I was eager to see the family members I hadn't seen in a while.

Partway there, Wes suggested I go to the wedding without him. I was stunned! Aghast! Angry! This was a family wedding, and I expected him to go with me. We discussed the issue the remainder of the trip. He didn't change his mind, and I didn't, either.

We arrived at his parents' home and greeted them, a visiting brother, and a guest. To my amazement, Wes brought up the topic at dinner. Suddenly, everyone was bantering back and forth about what Wes should do. So much for privacy! The next thing I knew, someone was calling for a vote: "Who thinks Wes should go to the wedding with Connie?" (The vote was zero—I was so stunned I *forgot to vote!) "Who thinks he should stay here?" (Basically the rest of the group.)*

I sat in disbelief, wondering what kind of family I'd married into. How dare they so freely air their opinions about matters that didn't involve them? I had temporarily forgotten that Wes had actually invited their input.

My family kept private matters private. You won't find us discussing who we voted for, how much money someone makes, how much a new car (or anything else) costs, or whether someone should attend a cousin's wedding! Wes continues to be amazed at our tight-lipped approach. He says my family redefines "private affairs."

When two people marry, they bring with them their own traditions and patterns. This often creates conflict—to say the least! And when the "conflict" is an opinionated mother-in-law who lives under your roof, things can become rather interesting, rather quickly!

My husband and I were involved in Marriage Ministries International for thirteen years and taught premarital classes for eight years before that—and knowing what we know now, we never would have counseled ourselves to marry thirty-eight years ago!

We're thankful that our ways aren't God's ways and that His wisdom prevailed. We married for all the wrong reasons. To sum it up, we were "two ticks looking for a dog"! We never found the "dog," but during our search for happiness, Jesus turned our hearts inside out for Him and began the lifelong process of remolding our character. And one of the "tools" He used was most unusual!

"Mom Reilly" came to live with us at the age of seventy-nine after living alone as a widow for fifteen years. We had been married for nine years and had four small children. "Mom" was determined to get as much attention as possible from my busy doctor husband, who was rarely home. She would rise early—four or five in the morning—and start banging a spoon on the kitchen table, announcing that it was time for her coffee.

She insisted on never being alone, which meant I couldn't even go to the bathroom alone. *"Diaaaane,"* followed by knocks on the door, could be heard throughout the house. Carpools were not immune to her, either. She became a fixture in the front passenger seat—with her hand on the horn if I walked a child inside and took too long. She was also a *joy* to shop with. When buying school clothes, I would find a comfy chair for her in the shoe department before heading out. Ten minutes later, I would inevitably hear my name paged over the loudspeaker system!

When Mom moved in, Bob and I had recently changed churches and found one that was filled with the joy of the Lord. We were in church almost every time the doors were open, and everyone in our family was growing spiritually. Bible studies on marriage were especially important because we knew little about God's blueprint for marriage. A "quiet and gentle" spirit I did *not* have, but desperately wanted—and needed!

I was in daily turmoil over the increasing demands I tried to place on myself in an effort to be the perfect wife and mother, with my "thorn," Mom Reilly, burrowing deeper and deeper into my side. Her tongue was so sharp; nothing I said or did pleased her. I became compliant on the outside, but seethed with resentment and anger on the inside. She was my "ball and chain." I took out my frustrations on my patient husband, sideswiping him time and again about being a workaholic. My tongue became as virulent as—if not worse than—Mom's.

A friend called from the East Coast one night, wrongly supposing we were three hours later rather than earlier. So, wide awake at 3:00 A.M., I decided to spend the next hour with the Lord. God met me in a powerful and unexpected way. I was reading the crucifixion story in John's Gospel. Jesus is on the cross looking down at His mother and His beloved disciples. With great tenderness and compassion, He says to John, "Here is your mother."[20] Tears filled my eyes and my heart burned as my Lord said to *me,* "Here is your mother." He was giving me *His* mother—to love and care for—just as He had given His mother to John. Was I not also a disciple? Was I not also commanded to love others as He had loved me?

My heart changed that night. God gave me His heart for Mom Reilly. No longer was it an effort to love and care for her. She lived with us for sixteen years, and we now see her time with us as a divine gift to bring supernatural love into our family. It was the Lord who asked for a gentle and quiet spirit from me—and it was this thorn of adversity that caused me to learn how to walk in the Spirit and not in the flesh. I fell more and more in love with Jesus—and my husband—as I practiced on "His mom." And as my heart changed toward Bob and he was no longer battling my angry and critical spirit, we began studying, applying, and then teaching God's blueprint for marriage.

One of the best things we did was to begin praying together. Our times together with the Lord are our most intimate. It's hard to be angry, critical, or disinterested when you go into the throne room together. We pray together daily and communion is so sweet. We also honor Mom Reilly and thank God for her, His special gift. From the bottom of my heart I can say that she gave us far more than we gave her.

I (Connie) had an awakening when God showed me that if I was one with Wes, then his parents should, in a sense, be my parents. They'd never take the place of my parents, of course, and I'd never share with them my many wonderful childhood memories, but in the sense of honor and regard, they were to be as my parents. I had never treated them poorly—in fact, I'd always tried to treat them well. However, I now wanted to elevate that to a higher standard.

Loving your in-laws is one of the dearest ways you can show love to your husband. So often, women share with us that their in-laws just aren't lovable. Those seemingly unlovable people are often the ones who need love the most! "If all you do is love the lovable, do you expect a bonus? Anybody can do that.... Live generously and graciously toward others, the way God lives toward you."[21]

Isn't this the way you want to live? Isn't this the way you want to love?

On a scale of 1 – 10, with 10 being "very well," how do you treat your in-laws?

"Mommy, Why Are You Always Mad at Daddy?"

Be Careful—the Apple Doesn't Fall Far from the Tree

JEAN BISHOP

One of our beloved role models is a woman who is fast approaching eighty. She walks either supported on the arm of her husband of almost sixty years, or pushing a walker. She may just now need assistance in her physical walking, but she long ago accepted assistance from her heavenly Father in her spiritual walk. She learned two big lessons: Only God is able to change the behavior of another, and when you point your finger at another's shortcomings, four fingers are pointing back at you.

Sometimes a child's guileless remark uncovers the fact that you have a problem! All four of Jean's children are actively involved in ministry. Would they be if their mother had stayed angry?

When Jack and I were first married, it truly did seem like what most girls dream about. We had a cute little apartment and both worked, and our lives were full and busy. After six months we bought an old house. After our first child was born, we decided I would no longer work outside the home. Jack worked eight to five, so I knew right when he would get home for dinner. Cindy and I would be all cleaned up and sitting on the porch waiting for Daddy. It was fun.

After a few more years, we had Nancy and David and built a lovely new home. Jack decided to go into business for himself, which meant no more steady income, lots of expenses, and long hours. The pressure and stress on our marriage increased dramatically.

Six years after starting the business, we had Melanie. I knew that starting a business was difficult, but so was being a homemaker and mother to four children! We had no automatic appliances or air conditioning, cooking *really* meant cooking, and most of the family responsibilities fell to me. Jack's "schedule" was nonexistent. He had to be at the store six days a week, all day long! I had the right to have a pity party…right?

Let me interject right here that we never had any thought of giving up on our marriage. We loved one another and enjoyed any time we could have together, but I didn't like what Jack was doing. Our marriage certainly wasn't like a storybook romance anymore.

One evening, Jack came home late as usual, and *as usual* I started my normal whining and haranguing: "Why are you late again? Why can't you ever be on time for dinner? You must waste time earlier in the day and then we have to suffer." You name it, I said it.

Then one of the children looked at me and said, "Why are you always mad at Daddy?" It was like a slap in the face. I was stunned! After all, it was *his* fault. Why blame me for being angry? I don't recall what my reply was, but I'm sure it was self-serving.

Almost immediately the Holy Spirit spoke to me: "When you stand before your heavenly Father, He will not ask you about Jack's shortcomings, but He will ask you about your attitudes and responses."

Wow! Even though he interrupts our schedule and upsets our lives, I'm supposed to be loving and kind and supportive?

The Holy Spirit answered me sweetly, "Yes."

I didn't hear an audible voice, but in my heart I knew I had received a rebuke from the Lord and it was my responsibility to make things right. I didn't change overnight, but with the Lord's help it was a beginning point. That encounter has never left me, and when I begin to step over the line, I ask Him to take control and bring me back. I learned that the blame game has no place in a marriage.

As the years have accumulated and we have grown in love and respect for one another, Jack has become more considerate of my needs, and I have learned to sense his frustrations. I've learned to stop thinking of myself and my "rights." I know one thing for certain—I have no right to be anything less that Christlike in every aspect of my life. An old hymn says, "Stamp Thine own image deep on my heart."[22] That's my prayer—for myself and for every woman reading this book.

Anger can erode the best of relationships. This didn't happen to Jean because she acknowledged that she had a problem and asked for God's help.

We recently sat behind Jean and Jack at a conference. Each time the speaker shared something humorous, Jean would smile and look at Jack, taking in his laughter. Surely she is thankful to God for helping her see where she needed to change and giving her the grace to start anew and leave her angry ways behind her. And surely her children—and grandchildren—are thankful as well!

Are you an angry woman?
If so, what will you do to change?

Little Eyes Are Watching

The Kids See Dad How Mom Sees Him

GERRI SHOPE

henever I (Connie) take communion, I always break the bread or cracker into two pieces before placing it in my mouth. It causes me to think about how Jesus' body was broken for my sins—not someone else's, but mine. When I break the bread with my own hands, it somehow becomes more real to me. I've been doing this for years. I don't even remember when I started, but I've never said a word about it to anyone.

When our twins were old enough to share in communion, I noticed that before they placed the crackers in their mouths, they broke them in two.

"Why do you do that, girls?"

"Because you do, Mom," they said, "so we do it that way, too."

I had no idea they'd even noticed. Our children take their cues—good and bad—from us.

My husband is the kindest, gentlest, and most easygoing person I know. Even when he came home from work and could barely find a clear spot on the living room floor to put down his foot because of all the toys, he never complained. He would just join in the fun or help clean up.

The good qualities I brought to the relationship were encouragement, motivation, and organization. I was the one who kept track of the details that kept the family running. I was the head cheerleader! I cheered everyone on and motivated them to do what needed doing.

My husband's easygoing ways made it hard for him to make decisions and get things done. I tried to motivate him, but my cheerleading quickly turned into nagging. This arrangement seemed to work for us. I took over some of the responsibilities he wasn't getting to, and he said that he probably needed my nagging.

Although this arrangement worked for a time, it wasn't in line with God's plan for marriage. It also had serious implications for our children. I didn't realize it, but they saw my overzealous "motivating" of their dad as a sign of disrespect. If I wasn't treating their dad in a respectful way, why should they?

Something had to be done, but I wasn't sure what. I turned to God. My prayer sounded something like, *God, please help*. No, not profound—but you don't have to be profound to talk to God! The process began with me learning not to say everything that came into my head. God gave me that tiny fraction of time after a thought came into my head to decide if I wanted to say it. I'd like to say that I always made the right choice, but old habits die hard.

I also stopped jumping in to "save the day" and allowed some things to go undone if they weren't my responsibility. My husband eventually got around to what needed to be done without me "motivating" him. As a result, the tension level in our household decreased.

How has this impacted our children's lives and how they see their dad? They are grateful for a more peaceful home and have come to appreciate their dad's strengths. Respect is no longer a stranger; whenever I treat my husband with regard, my children do as well.

I grieve the lost years! But I'm thankful for the fresh start the Lord provided—and continues to provide—day after day. When you choose to respect your husband, you'll discover he is blessed, you are blessed, *and* your children are blessed as well. Your decision will influence future generations because your kids will take with them what they saw lived out at home. This trickle-down effect—whether good or bad—will filter through countless generations. Why not do all you can to make sure what trickles down isn't just good, but great!

Gerri has been a "through thick and thin" kind of friend to me (Connie) for almost fifteen years. What I admire more than anything is her desire to do what's right in God's eyes.

*Gerri saw firsthand that the primary influencer of how the kids see dad is... guess who? Mom! The way she views her husband and the manner in which she treats him is very often mirrored by her children. A woman is counted wise if she carefully builds her house—and this includes her husband's reputation. However, she is counted a fool if she tears her home down with her own hands.*23

Don't be a foolish woman! Invest in your husband's stock—especially in front of your children. It will stay with them for a lifetime and will significantly alter the way they see Dad.

How is your husband's reputation at your house?

First Things First!

Getting the Cart Before the Horse Isn't a Good Thing,
Especially in Matters of the Heart!

KATHY JULIAN

*W*hen I (Connie) was a little girl, my sisters and I often visited our mother's parents, who lived just down the road. Grandma's kitchen was tiny and cramped, but that didn't prevent her from turning out some of the best food known to man. Or to little girls!

She often made apple pies and could peel the skins, from the apples in one long strip, never breaking the strip. This amazed us. But what she did next was even more amazing. Normally the picture of practicality and cleanliness, she would throw the skins over her shoulder and let it fall to the floor. Once it did, we'd all rush to see what letter it most resembled in its fallen state. According to Grandma, whatever letter it was would be the first letter of the name of the boy we would one day marry.

An old wives' tale? Of course! Even then we knew it was, but we still had fun playing along with Grandma. We couldn't wait for her to peel another apple and throw the peeling to see what our other options were! It was fun to dream.

Little girls have always been dreamers. And when it comes to dreaming, it's important to put first things first.

Do you remember what it was like to dream about your wedding as a little girl? Weddings have everything little girls like: music, a dress, a ring, flowers, cake, a beautiful bride (who is perfect), and a handsome groom (who is perfect.) Everything is perfect.

I longed to grow up and have my dream fulfilled. Over time, however, many of my illusions gave way to disillusionment. I became a teenager. Life was more painful and less beautiful than my childhood had been. While learning to walk through the turbulent real world, I hung on to that one childhood dream: marriage.

Though I dated, I never really had a boyfriend. My standard was high—perfection—and everyone seemed to fall short. I was okay with that because I still had my dream. Someday Mr. Perfect would show up.

One day during my freshman year of college, as I sat in the cafeteria, *he* walked in, making quite an entrance. Everyone in the cafeteria seemed to watch him. He was dashing and had a commanding presence as he went from table to table, talking to his many friends. Somewhere deep inside, I was being swept away, although I never thought I'd be a part of his life.

Not long after, Blake began paying attention to me and we began dating. I couldn't believe it! I was convinced that he was the one. But as quickly as the relationship started, it came to a crushing end. I was heartbroken. Mr. Perfect wasn't perfect and neither was I. Suddenly I felt very alone. I didn't want to give up on my dream of perfect love, but I began to wonder if it was actually possible.

Over the next year my heart remained broken and I felt uncertain about everything. I was a mess! I didn't realize it at the time, but Someone was gradually mending my heart. He was slowly picking up the pieces and putting them back together. He was teaching me that life was a gift from Him. He was teaching me to love again and to be loved.

This time, however, it wasn't a man who was teaching me to love. *It was my Savior.* I had grown up in a Christian home and been taught that God must be number one in my life. Now I was learning what that meant: "But seek first his kingdom and his righteousness, and all these things will be given to you as well."[24] I finally understood my childhood dream. And it wasn't silly; it had been given to me by God. The Bible talks about God as the groom and His church as the bride. He knows everything about me—my sins, my flaws, my inadequacies. Yet He stood by me patiently, healing my wounds and loving me unconditionally.

A few years later, I met my husband. We fell in love. He had so many of the qualities I wanted in a man. And he was flawed, just like I was. I realized that and accepted it…and he did, too.

We have been married almost twelve years. I'd like to say that our marriage is perfect. It's not! Sometimes life is all too real and painful. But I seek to live each day loving and being loved by God. He gives me the grace to love my husband—not change him, not disrespect him, but love him, help him, forgive him.

"Seek first his kingdom and his righteousness." When you seek God first and foremost, the "rest of the story" has a way of taking care of itself!

Kathy's husband, Kent Julian, coauthored the book How to Get Your Teen to Talk to You *with me (Connie) earlier this year.*

On the dedication page, Kent wrote:

> *To Kathy—*
> *My best friend and soul mate.*
> *You are absolutely incredible,*
> *and I'm the luckiest man on earth!*

Kathy is who she is because she chose to seek God first and trust Him to add anything else He wanted in her life. He added Kent to her life, as well as a darling young son and adorable twin daughters.

Kathy sought God. She is a God-seeker. We can't think of anything better to be!

Are you a God-seeker?

In Process with Prince Charming

Why Do Adoring Fiancées So Often Turn into Disgruntled Wives?

CAROLINE FENDLEY

So often, what we saw as our husband's strengths during the engagement, we then see as weaknesses once we become wives!

"He's so practical" often turns into "He's so frugal!"

"He's a perfectionist and I admire that" quickly becomes "He's a perfectionist and it drives me crazy!"

"He's such a deep thinker" is later viewed as "I wish he'd stop thinking and talk to me!"

"He loves to cook and we have so much fun in the kitchen" later transforms into "He's so messy. I wish he'd just leave my kitchen alone."

Do you sometimes feel like your Prince Charming has gotten back on his horse and ridden away? Maybe he no longer brings you flowers as regularly as he once did, but chances are, the Prince Charming you married is still there, if you just take a moment to find him!

Jeff and I were older when we married—twenty-eight and thirty. By the time we said "I do," both of us knew enough about life that neither expected the perfect mate. I had long given up on finding Prince Charming. And even if I did find that "perfect" man, he wouldn't be interested in me since I wasn't perfect.

I was attracted to Jeff because he was humble, kind, and committed to God. He accepted me for who I was. I didn't have to perform to gain his approval. I didn't have to be the most beautiful or talented or witty. We still had our issues to work through!

We came from different backgrounds and had to learn to accept those differences. Jeff is content with the basics of life. What matters to him is if something, such as a piece of furniture, is functional. What matters to me is how attractive it is. To him, a vacation means walking forty blocks in New York City and seeing every sight. I would prefer more relaxation. He is neat and orderly. I am…not!

When we married, I was working with a woman who had been a missionary on a remote island. God used her to disciple me through her living example of walking closely with Him each day. One main theme always emerged from our time together: *"God is gracious. You can trust Him."* Her words made a deep impression on my life.

She shared that God doesn't give us insight into other people's faults so we can criticize them, but so we can pray for them. Jeff and I tell each other when we think the other person is wrong or if our feelings are hurt, and usually we can work it out. But occasionally, he just can't seem to come around to my way of thinking or won't admit that he's wrong (when I know I'm right!). When conflict can't be resolved, I pray that God would give us oneness on the matter. It's amazing to see the Lord answer this prayer. Sometimes He changes Jeff's attitude; sometimes mine.

Oddly enough, one factor that has increased our commitment to each other is that neither of us came from Christian families. This has caused us to appreciate each other even more. Having a Christian mate who shares the same values and beliefs is a treasure of inestimable worth.

The second person God has used to teach me is Elisabeth Elliot. In her teaching she often speaks about acceptance and says, "We're to trust God, even when things don't seem fair or make sense." I've also heard her say, "In acceptance lies peace." When I'm struggling with finding fault, the Lord often brings this to mind and I'm reminded that I can't change other people. God made them the way they are, with their own unique personalities. Fretting and worrying only make things worse: "Do not fret, it leads only to evil."[25] It leads *only* to evil, nowhere else.

Another minefield I have learned to navigate is the tendency to compare Jeff with other husbands. This is so destructive. Some women's husbands lavish gifts on them or plan romantic getaways. Jeff is thrifty and doesn't operate that way. I've learned to appreciate the other things he does, such as being a tremendous help around the house and with the boys. It's a valuable gift because I can't do it alone (I have some health problems that cause me to have a low energy level).

Jeff accepts me as I am. It's a two-way street—lots of give-and-take. As someone said, "It's so simple, but not easy." That's because we have an enemy who wants to defeat us. Too often, we look at failures and imperfections. If we're not careful, Satan can get a foothold and cause discontent. In Romans 1, one of the sins that Paul mentions is being unthankful. When we're critical of our husbands, we are being ungrateful for what God has given us.

I don't have one "best thing" I ever did for my marriage because all of life is a growing process. I still have lots of room to grow, but by God's grace, I eagerly look forward to the coming days and years with my Prince Charming!

Caroline shows tremendous wisdom in accepting her husband for who he is. Acceptance is such a big deal! I (Connie) remember the first time I ever really "saw" the message in Romans 15:7: "Accept one another, then, just as Christ accepted you, in order to bring praise to God." I was deeply convicted as I read those words. I accepted almost everyone so easily—except for Wes. The Lord impressed on my heart that I needed to accept him...not to do so is to actually deflect praise from Him. And who wants to do that? So I asked the Lord to forgive me and to help me begin accepting Wes just the way he was, which is wonderful. I'd just been overlooking some of the wonder!

How do you feel about the days ahead with your Prince Charming? If a man is accepted, his Prince Charming colors are far more apt to show.

Does your life praise God in the way you accept your husband?

More than "Just a Wife"

A Man Holds Such a Tender Place in His Wife's Heart When the Marriage Begins, but Soon Seems Just a Whisper Above a Stray Animal.

ANONYMOUS

Every morning, barring bad weather, I (Connie) go for a run in a nearby park. I often bump into a woman and her two small dogs, Roger and Rachel. Roger is a chubby black terrier and Rachel is a pudgy white poodle. Both are as wide as they are tall. This woman has Roger and Rachel trained to perfection. Whenever we get close to one another on the path, the woman shouts the command "Ignore!" and the dogs literally turn on a dime and go sit at her feet. It's pretty impressive. (We had a dog once who never understood a single command, other than "Do whatever you'd like. You own the home.")

But one day Roger decided to ignore his master's command. When he saw me coming, he started running toward me at full speed. She must've said "ignore" two hundred times in a span of thirty seconds—she sounded like a machine gun—but Roger felt *like living dangerously that day, for he continued to run in my direction. His owner went ballistic.*

"Roger, when I say 'ignore,' I mean 'ignore.' Why chase her anyway? She's just a runner." She picked Roger up and headed for her car. No doubt about it, Roger was in the doghouse!

Her words stayed with me: "Why chase her? She's just a runner." What was that supposed to mean? Just a runner? Compared to what? A squirrel? A rabbit? Another dog? I'll never know. But "just a runner" implied that I was lacking something. You can't be thin-skinned around this place!

Later, I thought about how this episode could apply to my wife life. Too often I'm content being "just a wife," rather than striving for excellence and godliness in my marriage. The way to stop being just a wife and become a woman who delights God isn't difficult— if your Makeover Artist is God.

There are actually three "best things" I did for my marriage:

- I invited Jesus into it.
- I learned what my job description as a wife was.
- I committed to obedience in my daily walk.

When I asked my husband his opinion about the best thing I ever did for our marriage (I was hoping he could come up with *something!*), he said, "You learned how to really be a wife." To my surprise, he followed that statement with all the benefits and blessings he'd received because of this.

I had learned "how to really be a wife" through a study I took with a friend. I'd been married for twenty-four years and had known Jesus for five of them. This class was supposed to teach you what a wife's "job description" was. I agreed with the "job" part of it—being married was hard work! My friend and I looked into the class, discovered there was no homework, and decided to give it a go.

I must admit, my motives weren't pure. I was more excited about being with friends than about learning anything. And the fact that there was no homework was right up my alley. It seemed like a perfect match for my fun-loving personality.

I didn't say anything to my husband—I didn't want to be scrutinized or have to live up to any expectations he might have. As the weeks rolled by, I heard the words *submit, obey,* and *helper,* which actually sounded more like *cater to, wait on,* and *serve.* This wasn't what I was after when I signed up for the class! Yet I found that I was listening and learning in spite of myself. Truth has a way of wooing you even when you don't really want to be wooed. My biggest obstacle, however, was that I wanted to know if there was something in it for me. If I were to change, I wanted something in return.

Each week, I learned more and more about being a godly wife, but it seemed like the wife was doing all the work. I think the teacher read my mind because her next words were: "Don't worry about what your husband is or isn't doing. That's between God and him. Concern yourself with your own behavior—that's what you're responsible for." Foiled again!

I began to learn things I'd never known. For instance, when I submit to my husband, I'm really submitting to God. What an incredible thought! Did that mean if I didn't submit to my husband, I was refusing to submit to God as well?

I also learned that when I obey God, I position myself under His protective umbrella. Sounds so simple, doesn't it?

Once I obey, the responsibility for that obedience is His. Now there's a freeing thought. Did this mean I didn't have to keep all the balls in the air all the time?

Then one day the question was asked: "Have you ever invited Christ into your marriage?" Well, probably not. Our marriage wasn't terrible, but it could definitely use a Savior.

I took this class three consecutive semesters—same class, same teaching. But I still wasn't quite ready to give up my old ways. Old ways can be so comfortable! Finally, though, as I started the class for the third time, it was as if I woke up. I was tired of living just "somehow." I was tired of being "just a wife" in whatever manner suited me for the day. I was ready to pursue holiness and righteousness.

Ephesians 5:22 was constantly on my mind: "Wives, submit to your husbands as to the Lord." So whenever my husband asked me to do something I didn't want to do, I would pray, *Lord, this is for You.* I began to see how freely I served my children—and even my friends. But I rarely treated my husband in the same manner. And when I did, it was as if I were tossing him a crumb. Never did he receive my best.

I stopped making all the decisions involving the kids and began including my husband. This wasn't easy, but it was time to give him the role that should have been his all along. It's amazing to see how he has stepped into this role once there was an opening! I do all I can to help him succeed in this role rather than waiting in the wings, ready to step in if he stumbles.

It was also time to move him back up the ladder of my heart—the children were far above him in my love and affections. I asked God to forgive me and to help me give my husband his rightful place. Did the kids resent this? No! They loved seeing me treat their dad in such a manner.

I wish I knew this twenty-six years ago…I think about the time I wasted. But God's plan and timing are perfect, so I have stopped the "I wishes" and "what ifs," and each day I ask God to help me…and He always does.

I stand in constant awe at what God has done in molding this glob of clay! This is a whole new way of life for me. I missed out on it for twenty-six years, but I'm eternally thankful that I didn't miss out on it a second longer. I look forward with joy and great expectation to what He continues to do in me as He blesses and directs my life.

Don't you marvel that even after twenty-six years, hearts and marriages can be changed if a woman purposes to change? And the key is obedience. Sometimes when we think of obedience, we think of frisky puppies that need to go to obedience school. Or maybe we think of two-year-old toddlers who need molding and training. But how often do we think of us?

Obedience is all about us! Obedience is the key that opens the door to being more than "just a wife." It's what will get you on track and keep you on track. It's your ticket to being a woman in whom the Lord delights!

Our friend has now taken about half her neighborhood to this study—and she's working on the other half! She doesn't want any of her friends to miss out on the incredible blessings that occur when a woman purposes to be more than "just a wife."

And you don't want to miss out, either!

Aren't you ready to be more than "just a wife"?

Lay Down That Fishing Pole!

*A Man's Hopes and Dreams Shouldn't
Be Squelched by the Woman He Loves*

KELLI WESTPHALL

*W*hen *a man is an adventurer and risk taker and his
wife is Stable Mabel, you can almost smell the conflict that might
arise. The adventurer is always ready for the next mountain to
climb…the next job to pursue. The call of the wild is in his blood.
The more "out there" the plan, the more his creative juices are
stirred. His motto is "I can do anything! Let's do it!" He doesn't
even need to know what the big picture is, he'll just figure it out
along the way.*

*But his wife…she wants stability. Kelli's story is so encourag-
ing. Leaving her comfort zone, she nurtured and supported her
husband's passions. She gives us the opportunity to be a fly on the
wall and watch God's plan unfold.*

I gave birth to John-Luc in a hospital twenty miles north of
Paris to the sounds of a French midwife yelling, "Zee baby eez

coming, Madame! It eez zee moment for le pushing!" Eighteen months later, we returned to the United States for a visit. Our first morning there, John-Luc refused to let me put milk on his cereal.

"What's the problem here, buddy? It's just regular milk." He had his doubts. After all, he'd never seen this white substance in a plastic jug. As far as he knew, milk came in a one-liter rectangular blue and white cardboard box that had a shelf life of eighty years! It only went into the fridge after you opened it. It was several days before he accepted the new version.

John-Luc is Steady Eddy—"Why change? Let's get the routine down and stick to it"—just like his mom.

Our firstborn son, five-year-old Christopher, is the opposite. Recently, coming back to the States for a visit, I asked Christopher how he felt about moving back to France the next month. Since I was filled with uncertainties about our return, I prepared myself for an outpouring about why he too might be apprehensive.

Christopher replied, "I wish we were moving tomorrow."

Horrified, I asked why.

"Well, I know my new friends can't wait to meet me." *What else is out there? What's coming up next? You're fun…but who else will I meet tomorrow?* Christopher is just like his dad.

My father is a professional fisherman, and even though I was never attracted to the sport, my early years of marriage felt like I was trying to reel in a swordfish with a cane pole (can *you* do that, Dad?) when it came to dealing with my husband. Lee's interests were vast and varied, and change exhilarated him. His networking skills and desire to "see what's out there" led him to jobs in radio, television, audio production, landscaping, and retail management. During his off-hours he helped with high school ministry at church, built sets for plays at the school where I taught, and was involved in community and church drama. Lee's sense of adventure kept life exciting.

But it also caused frustration. I remember saying, "Honey, you can't do *everything!*" It was that old Eve thing. I wanted the one thing that Lee couldn't give me: a sense of routine and stability. So I decided I would take matters into my own hands. I figured it was my role as his wife to reel him in. I tried to keep our life normal and safe.

In May of 1992, we received a call from a longtime friend. "Are you guys still serious about serving overseas?" he asked.

Both of us had been involved in short-term missions during our college years and felt sure that we would serve overseas in a full-time capacity at some point. "Yes!" Jeff replied.

"Well, you need to fly down to Orlando this weekend and meet the director. He's just here for a few days."

I quickly explained to Lee why it was impossible for me to go. "I've got fifty elementary kids signed up for a drama workshop this weekend."

Because everything is a possibility for Lee (and God), he said, "Kelli, we both need to be there if this is what God has for us. I'll get the tickets." And through a series of miraculous events, we got the last two tickets on that Friday's flight—right next to each other!

Everything came together, and we've lived overseas since 1993. And during those years, God has continued to remind me to put down my fishing pole. God made Lee a dreamer and a doer, and while my input is vital, I don't want to hold us back from what God may have for us just because of my dislike of change.

Last year I attended a conference and was assigned to write a love letter to my spouse. In the brainstorming process I wrote a list of the things I was most thankful for: our boys, our ministry in France, our years of missions, the women who have impacted my life, the growth in my spiritual journey through transitions and conflicts. Suddenly I realized that the greatest experiences of my life have been a result of God placing me with Lee! I was not created as a risk taker, but Lee was, and as I embrace that quality in him I've sensed God's immense pleasure and blessing.

Recently I took a spiritual gifts survey. According to the test, I have the gift of faith. What a match! Lee is out there with a vision of how God wants to use our family, and God has placed me by Lee's side to have the faith to see Him accomplish it.

Just the other day we drove by a wooded pond area that's right on the edge of the French village where we now live. Lee's extended gaze onto the water was followed by an idea: "Why don't we all go fishing this weekend?"

I thought, *Hmm, my fishing pole is tucked away in the closet at the moment. I think I'll stay home and sip on a cup of coffee. That's one adventure I'll let the guys have together.*

Kelli's invisible fishing pole—the one she used to reel in Lee—is tucked away as well. There is nothing wrong with giving your opinions to your husband, but if God has placed a passion on his heart, support it! Lee stood firm in God's plan for him. And now Kelli is seeing with eyes of faith that God has called Lee to be a fisher of men, and she is right by his side sharing in their ministry. How draining and defeating it must be for a man to have every dream squelched because of an overzealous wife's desire for personal secu-

rity. Kelli has shown us that when she exercised her faith in God, He gave her everything she needed to support His call on her husband's life.

Do you help your husband dream big?

"Help! I Don't Know What I'm Doing!"

When You've Been Captain of the Boat, It's Hard to Let Go of the Wheel

ANONYMOUS

The origins of names are fascinating, aren't they?

Do you know where the S.O.S on the little scrubby pad came from? The scrubbers were invented in 1917, by cookware peddler Edwin Cox, who handed them out as free gifts to get his foot in the door with prospective customers. The gifts went over well, since most women had to deal with food stuck to their pans. Cox, who manufactured the pads in his own kitchen, asked his wife to help him name the product. Mrs. Cox suggested S.O.S, as in "save our saucepans," and the name stuck![26]

Ever wonder where the word helper *first appears in the Bible? Maybe you didn't even know it was there! It's in Genesis 2 right after God creates man. Adam is alone, which God deems "not good." So He creates a helper for him—woman! You!*

Helper *is more than just a word. It's a high and holy title. It's not about something you do…it's about who you are as a wife. Perhaps this is news to you. It was to a friend of ours.*

I came into marriage assuming many things, most of which I discovered were far from reality! One thing I assumed was that everything would be teamwork and that we would split things 50/50. I quickly learned that this wasn't true—at least from my viewpoint! Unfortunately, as the years went by I concentrated on what my husband did wrong and found myself constantly wanting to "fix" him.

His work required a lot of travel, which left me in charge of everything at home. Where was the teamwork? I felt like a single parent with an occasional weekend husband. Over those years, two things were building up in me:

- Resentment of his schedule and his lack of help at home.
- Pride in myself. I was proud of what I could do without his help. I believed he needed me more than I needed him.

We rarely fought, and on the surface all seemed well. But my pride and resentment manifested itself in other ways—cutting words, silence, body language, a bad attitude. I felt so superior, yet I couldn't have been further from what God desired me to be in our marriage.

But God had plans for us. He first led me to an in-depth Bible study and eventually to a class specifically on being a godly wife. I was appalled to discover the numerous actions and attitudes of mine that were wrong. I had rationalized them for such a long time that they had become normal to me. I was "out of order" with God's plan for my life. I wasn't supposed to be the head of our home, which I'd taken such pride in. No, God gave this role to my husband, and I knew that God knew best.

God also showed me how I was to be a helper to my husband. At first I wasn't sure I liked this, but then I learned that the title of *helper* is precious—in fact, it's one God uses of Himself over and over again in Scripture. And if God said that's who I was to be as a wife, then that's who I wanted to be.

So I began to embrace my role as helper and started giving the leadership of our home *back* to my husband. And what a difference it made when I took my eyes off myself and my happiness and placed them on God and how I needed to live to please Him.

It hasn't been easy to change, but as I've worked to become my husband's helpmate, encourager, and cheerleader, the blessings have been amazing! Some may consider this old-fashioned and outdated, but it's not. It's God's perfect will for our lives. He called woman to be a helper to her husband *before* sin entered the world—when the world was still in its perfect state. It's hard to argue with that!

As I've begun to line up my life with God's order, doors to ministry that never would have opened five or ten years ago are now opening. Just recently, I asked my husband what he felt was the best thing I had done for our marriage. His quick reply was, "You're patient with me." Unbelievable! For so long, I was just the opposite. My heart has softened, and his has as well. Our marriage isn't perfect and we're still very different from each other, but there is a strong, loving bond between us because God has changed—of all people—me!

Is your life out of order, like our friend's was? Maybe it's been out of order for so long that you don't know how to even begin rearranging it. Start with a prayer as simple as this: Lord, my life is out of control. I'm overwhelmed. Will You help me start over? *Whatever* your prayer, know that He hears you and He'll help you start fresh.

When our friend aligned her life with God's Word, doors to ministry began to open. So often women wonder what God wants them to do with their lives. If you want to discover all He has for you, we suggest you get your "wife life" in order. It seems to springboard a woman to being greatly used by God.

Why not say a prayer today and begin calling your life to order?

In what ways do you resist God's best for your life?

Compromise Isn't for Sissies!

The women in the stories you're about to read could have dug in their heels and insisted on getting their own way, or they could have counted the cost and discovered what the higher calling in marriage really is. And (here's a hint) it's not getting your own way! Meet some "count the cost" women, and see how in giving a little they gained far more than they could have imagined possible.

The "Honey-Do" List

Blessed Is the Child Whose Mother Sees Dad as a Giant

THELMA COODY

*W*hen my (Connie) sisters and I were little, we used to ask my mother, "How do you know if you're in love?" We were much too young to be in love, but the very idea intrigued us. We'd watched plenty of black-and-white movies, and we'd seen firsthand how John Wayne and Cary Grant could virtually sweep a woman off her feet with barely a glance. "Does it really happen like that, Mom?" we'd ask.

We especially loved it when the hero kissed the heroine at the end of the movie. We took special notice if his kiss caused her leg to bend at the knee. Obviously there were kisses—and then there were kisses.

"Did your knee ever bend like that when Daddy kissed you?"

Our poor mother would blush and laugh and try to change the subject, but we weren't easily swayed! Our biggest fear was that love would come our way and we'd miss it. That would be dreadful—to never know the thrill of having your leg bend at just the right moment!

Sometimes after we'd gone to bed—snuggled under our electric blankets in the attic bedroom we shared—my sisters and I *would continue talking about love. Often our thoughts turned to our parents. The fact that they were extremely happy years after they said their vows didn't escape us. They might even (gasp!) still be in love.*

We wondered what it was like when they fell in love. Had Daddy swept Mom off her feet? Surely he had! If John Wayne—who was merely a pretend hero—could, then certainly Daddy could.

Years later, I asked Mom to share one of the things that has made her marriage so full and satisfying. I count it a great privilege to share my mother's story with you.

Homer and I were born the same year, 1932, within five miles of each other. I was born in my parents' home; Homer in his grandparents' home. Both of us grew up on farms and we live on one still. We went to rural grade schools. He was more "uptown" than I, as his was a two-room school and mine only one.

We met as freshmen and were friends throughout high school. We went together to both our junior and senior banquets. I wore the same dress both years—a pale pink one—but my mother and I altered the neckline my senior year to update it.

During our senior year, Homer and his family moved, which placed him on the same school bus as me. The long ride suddenly became more interesting! Toward the end of that year, our friendship took a serious turn. We graduated in May, became engaged in June, and married in September.

We both worked and our marriage was great. Two years later, during the Korean War, Homer was drafted. He was sent to England and my brother, who was an engineer, loaned me the money to travel and be with him after a few months. When his tour was over, we came home—bringing our newborn daughter with us. Twenty months later our second daughter was born, and eighteen months after that came a third! Things were rather busy in our home, but we were so happy. Seven years later, we added a fourth and final daughter to our family.

I was a full-time mother and Homer was a fireman—working twenty-four-hour shifts. He also farmed and ran a few head of cattle. Sometimes I'd ask him to perform "honey-do" jobs. His easygoing nature, coupled with his erratic schedule, meant those jobs might or might not get done immediately. Sometimes I would stew about this, but God finally got through to me that these little things didn't matter. They just weren't a big deal.

I began to look at all I had to be thankful for in Homer. He always found time for a front yard softball game with his girls. He'd take on all of them—never going to bat himself. Whoever wasn't batting would help him field. I suppose if you counted the hours he was out there with them, it would be in the hundreds. He taught them to play basketball as well. Years later, the girls played high school sports. Whether they won or lost, Homer was proud of them and never once put them down for a poor play, a missed free throw, or a strikeout. "Even the best hitters strike out sometimes," he'd tell the girls after a softball game. Or "If a player never fouls, she's not hustling much. Don't worry about those fouls." He always emphasized the positive and never made them feel badly about the way they played.

Homer spent endless hours running up and down our long driveway teaching them to ride a bicycle. When they fell off, he'd pick them up, brush them off, and help them get back on. He never let them quit after they fell. He was teaching them so much more about life than just riding a bicycle.

He once stopped his tractor and came in from the field to bring a baby rabbit to the house so his little daughters could see and feel it. I don't know who was more excited—Homer or the girls!

Every year he'd load us up and take us camping for a few days at a nearby lake. His preference would have been to stay home. He'd say to me, "I don't know why these girls enjoy camping so much. I grew up camping [he'd had no running water or electricity until he was almost eighteen years old, and no indoor toilet until we married], and that was plenty for me." But he knew how much the girls enjoyed it, so every summer off we'd go. He could have easily squelched their fun and refused to go—or sulked once we got there—but he didn't. In fact, it was many years before the girls knew how he really felt.

Homer especially loved Christmas. He'd never had much of a Christmas when he was a child, so each year he made sure the girls got something they really wanted: a Tiny Tears doll, a nurse's kit, a Barbie, an Etch-a-Sketch, a first watch. One year we bought them new bicycles. He spent hours putting them together in our cellar while they were at school. We even found small license plates with each of their names on them.

Most of all, Homer has always given of himself. He never missed any of their school or sporting events—even if they were one of the youngest on the team and had little chance of getting to play. He took us on drives on Sunday afternoons and showed us the best lights in town every Christmas season. He'd stop the car in front of their favorite displays and let them "watch" the lights for as long as they wanted. He was patient and kind, which is how love is described in the Bible.

Needless to say, these special memories he made with his family will last a lifetime and are much more important than whether he finished my honey-do jobs in a timely fashion. I'm so glad I learned to ease up and not fret about the small things. This freed me up to love him so much more and awakened in me an awareness of his many wonderful traits.

We recently celebrated our fifty-third wedding anniversary. Homer had quadruple bypass surgery in 1990, so every year is a bonus for us. We have thirteen grandchildren, and Homer continues making memories with them. They all adore him, and I do, too.

We are grateful for each day we enjoy together. God has blessed me with many wonderful friends, but Homer is my best friend. I'm thankful the Lord showed me that some things are not important and to look for the good qualities in your spouse. I've found that when I do this, I find so very many, and I know you will, too.

I share my story with you in the hopes that you won't spend your energies picking your husband apart. Focus instead on his good qualities. You'll be glad you did. And so will he!

And so will God!

If you asked my sisters and me who impacted our lives the most, I suspect each of us would say our dad. In our eyes, he was—and is—a giant.

But do you know who allowed him to be a giant to us? Our mother. Her legacy is that she allowed him to be "big" to us. And now she's doing that same thing for our children.

I had no idea Mom purposed early on to overlook the minor irritants that come along in every marriage. This is even more meaningful to me because she is a detail person who always makes sure the small things get done. So certainly it wasn't easy for her to let them go. Yet she did—because she didn't want anything to get in the way of her relationship with Daddy.

What do you suppose would happen if you began letting go of the small things in your marriage? What do you think might happen if your children heard you share something you admired about their dad? What if you did this every night for three weeks, which is how long it takes a new habit to develop? We suspect a whole new tone would be set in your home—one that you, and everyone else, will love.

My sisters and I consider ourselves doubly fortunate—for not only do we have a giant in our father, but we have just as much of a giant in our mother as well.

Are you a "recognizer of giants"?

When Mornings Aren't His Cup of Tea

No Man Enjoys Being One of His Wife's "Projects"

CHERYL BUCHANAN

*I*t seems that in every marriage one partner is a morning person—but usually only one! Morning people wake up bright and cheerful, ready to attack the day with a sunny sort of vengeance. They hum as they make the coffee, whistle as they collect the paper, and greet everyone in their path with a warm hello and maybe even a hug, proclaiming what a wonderful day it looks to be.

The other person in the marriage generally wakes up slowly—very slowly—and usually prefers to be left alone for a while. There is no humming, whistling, hugging, or proclamations of any kind. Wes once told me that he didn't feel like he was actually awake until at least ten in the morning. By then, I'd been up for hours and was ready for a nap!

In the early years of my marriage, I determined that I would turn Wes into a morning person if it was the last thing I ever did. I know that you non-morning people are probably irritated with me, and I'm sorry—I can only plead youthful ignorance. Well, Wes was about as receptive to this idea as a bear in hibernation might

be.... Maybe not even that much. But this didn't stop me from try-
ing. It wasn't long, though, before I had to admit that my project
was a failure. He simply wasn't interested in becoming like me!

It's a huge step for a woman to begin to understand that God
didn't wire her husband—or anyone else—in the same way He
wired her. And it's an even bigger step to realize that He often uses
these very differences to draw us closer to Himself.

The best thing I ever did for my marriage was to stop talking
to my husband first thing in the morning.

Mark has always been a deep thinker, with a multitude of
things mulling in his brain, but rarely is he thinking of the
things a wife considers important. I, too, am always thinking,
but rarely deep thoughts. I wake up most mornings with my
to-do list running through my head—appointments, schedules, various sundry tasks, all crowding in and making me
weary before I'm even fully awake. Like any good wife, from
the moment I opened my eyes I would begin to share all
these things with Mark. His response? He'd retreat to his
study to be alone, to contemplate in silence *not* my mundane
musings but the "complexities of life." I began to feel more
and more isolated. I longed for a husband who could fill my
deepest needs.

About six years ago, God put a longing in my heart to
discover more of Him and more of what He had for me. This
began a journey of realizing that there is only One who can
fill my deepest needs, and He is always present, attentive, listening, calling me to listen. The journey wasn't always easy,
but as God deepened my trust in Him, I knew that whatever
He asked me to do He would faithfully walk me through.

The first step of the journey was learning to listen. God

began to draw me into a deeply personal prayer life that was more listening than talking. As He poured out His love and acceptance to me, He began to purify my heart. His rebukes were stern but gentle and kind—a kindness that led to repentance. I spent over a year in constant repentance as His Spirit brought every thought, every action, every word into His light. He brought to mind sins from my past that had long been buried and unconfessed, and He brought healing, cleansing, and resolve. God did what I had hardly the faith to imagine: He redeemed my past and brought blessing through my obedience.

Through this time of repentance, God began to breathe new life into our marriage. As He began to change and purify me, it allowed me to communicate with Mark. Our conversations became more intimate, our needs more openly expressed. We studied together *The Five Languages of Love* by Gary Chapman (see the chapter called "Different Strokes for Different Folks"). For the first time in our marriage, I felt totally cherished.

Through my communion with God I have learned how to read Mark. He still often retreats inwardly when the pressures of being a pastor, author, and speaker accumulate, but I have learned not to take his withdrawal personally; instead, I lift him to God. God often shows me little ways to bless him, to help him see we're in this together, to let him know I love him and support him.

So the best thing I ever did for my marriage I continue to do every day: I speak few words to Mark first thing. Instead, I fill my early mornings talking—and listening—to the One in heaven who cherishes me. He fills me and shows me how to interact with the one on earth who cherishes me.

The turning point in Cheryl's marriage came when she realized that only One could fill her deepest needs, and it wasn't her husband. So often we place such pressure on our husbands to do what only God can do. If we do this for long, we'll become the very personification of bitterness.

Something wonderful happens in a woman's heart when she takes her eyes off of her husband and her circumstances and places them on the Lord. We know for a fact that God can turn hearts of stone into hearts of flesh.[27] His Word tells us that, and we can testify that it has occurred in our own lives.

If you're letting your differences with your mate eat away at you, you're headed to a place you don't want to go. Let go of thinking your ways are better than his. As you do, you'll find yourself moving in a different direction—you will have veered off the road to bitterness and onto the pathway to joy. And that's a trip worth taking.

Do you accept the gift of you and your spouse's differences,
or do you hold his differences against him?

An Issue You Can Sink Your Teeth Into

Cleanliness Isn't Always Next to Godliness

CYNDY SALZMANN

Have you ever had a friend whose name alone makes you smile? We do! Cyndy has been that kind of friend to us for many years. Her sense of humor is quicker than one of Tiger Woods's putts. But she can turn a conversation just as quickly and bring tears to your eyes with her deep insights.

Several years ago, Cyndy began studying how to become a godly wife. The first week was wonderful! The second week brought continued enthusiasm, but not quite as much as before. By the third week, she began to drag out the marriage material and ponder her three weeks of attempted change. Instead of completing her assignment, she wearily scrawled across the page she was working on something countless other women have only thought: "WHY SHOULD I?"

Cyndy's "problem" is the very same problem every woman faces. Old habits are comfortable, ruts are relaxing, and change is taxing. And being right somehow seems far more important than being righteous. Besides, does anyone really notice the little things we do?

❦

As I bare my soul for all to see, I can't help but wish that my story were a bit more spiritual— or at least normal! I'd love to say that the best thing I ever did for my marriage was whisking my husband off for surprise romantic weekends. Or perhaps sharing devotions each night before we drift off to sleep. Honestly, even folding his underwear would be better! But God knows how to get our attention, and for me it began as a battle of wills—mine versus His—at the bathroom sink.

You see, the best thing I ever did for my marriage was to quit spitting in my husband's sink. Your eyes aren't deceiving you. The turning point in my marriage happened while my mouth was full of toothpaste.

After John and I had been married a few years, we built a new home for our family. One of the amenities that particularly delighted John was the large master bathroom. Not only did it have a lot of space; it also had *two* sinks! But John saw these sinks as His and Hers, while I viewed them as free-for-all plumbing fixtures!

Not long after the moving cartons were unpacked, John noticed that I was using *his* sink to brush my teeth—and brazenly moving to the *her* side to apply makeup and style my hair. After patiently giving me the benefit of the doubt for a few weeks and attributing my use of his sink to unfamiliarity, John politely brought the matter to my attention.

I responded by laughing hysterically. "You have to be kidding!" After composing myself and noticing that he wasn't laughing, I said, "I'm the mother of your children! I should be able to spit anywhere I want!"

John responded by explaining that I had my "own" sink and he preferred that I didn't use his in the future. I lamely argued that the toothbrush holder was closer to his sink. "Then move it," he countered calmly as he left the room, confident that the matter was settled.

As you may have guessed, the matter was definitely *not* settled. This was no longer about dental hygiene—it was about being *right*. And as a card-carrying member of the Strong Will Society of America, I knew who was right—and it wasn't my sink-hogging husband! After all, who cleaned his sink?

As my righteous indignation began to subside, I thought, *Why upset the poor misguided man? After all, what he doesn't know won't hurt him.* I simply changed my morning routine so he wasn't around when I spit. Problem solved.

I continued this sink subterfuge for well over a year without even a pinprick of conscience. Then I began learning about my role as a wife and discovered it didn't include subterfuge! As I learned more about God's design for marriage, which includes submission to my husband, the Holy Spirit convicted me every time I spread toothpaste on my brush. I began to think that maybe I wasn't right (shocking!). The issue was no longer about His and Her sinks; it was about honoring God by submitting to the will of my husband (I *hated* this!). But I loved God—and my husband—so I began using the Her sink exclusively.

And everyone lived happily ever after, right? *No!* In fact, what was once a small matter became a huge spiritual battle each morning. I literally had to pull myself and my toothbrush away from my husband's sink. I would think, *It's so much easier to just use his sink. It's no big deal....* But I knew it really was a big deal. It was a matter of obedience. God was shaping me little by little into a vessel He could use for His glory. I needed to learn the hard but vital lesson of doing things His way. Each morning as I stood before the mirror with a mouthful of toothpaste, I would make the decision to spit in my own sink—and shout triumphantly in my heart, *This one's for You, Lord!*

Since the days of bathroom rebellion, God has opened incredible doors for me to serve Him. I so appreciate the protection and joy that come from obeying God. My children are growing up in a family that is committed to doing things God's way—even though we occasionally stumble along the way. I've been given opportunities to speak and write. Amazingly, as I write this chapter, I'm also at work on my third book. Just think, all this from adjusting to His and Her sinks!

Now…the answer to the question I bet you're just dying to know: Have I gotten used to the Her side of the vanity? No! It's still a battle, but these days it's a sweet battle. God has taught me that each time I make a decision to walk in obedience, I get to enjoy the pleasure of walking hand in hand with Him. And this always brings a sparkle to my smile!

"Who's watching, anyway?" is the question we posed at the beginning of Cyndy's story. Well, someone was watching! Cyndy's daughter Anna happened to stroll by just after she'd written "Why should I?" at the bottom of her lesson. Later, as Cyndy and Anna were getting ready for the day, Cyndy told Anna to go to the bathroom and brush her teeth. For the first time in her life, Anna asked her mom, "Why should I?" As Cyndy was about to say, "Because I said so, that's why!" it dawned on her that she was being observed as well by her heavenly Father, who could actually respond to her in the same way.

Attitudes are contagious! Little girls and boys absorb life lessons so easily. Is spitting in your husband's sink when you've been asked not to a big deal? You might be tempted to offer an emphatic "No!" But that's really not true at all, is it…

How quick are you to respond to your husband's simple requests, even when they make no sense to you?

The Defining Moment

Two Minds Are Better than One...Most of the Time

BARB SNYDER

One of the best things about being with my (Nancy) sister, Christine, is that I barely have to think when we're together. She and I are so much alike that we are often mistaken for twins. Our voices are so similar that my children can't distinguish who is speaking to them when we phone while on a trip. And we often respond in unison to whoever is speaking to us.

You can imagine what Christine's and my conversations are like. I'll begin to say something and she'll finish my thought. This is so much fun and is one of my favorite things about being with her. I do this for her as well. We find this highly amusing since we have identical senses of humor. We're together only a few times a year, as I live in Nebraska and she lives in Texas. Now that I think about it, it might get a wee bit wearisome if we lived together and were always completing each other's thoughts. It did for Barb Snyder's husband, Chuck.

When Chuck and I married forty-seven years ago, he didn't have a clue that he wouldn't be able to finish a thought for the next thirty-three years.

I loved Chuck's quiet spirit. He listened to me, and I enjoyed talking. He was thrilled that I was outgoing and could talk easily with anyone. These were traits that drew us to each other.

I came from a family that talked about everything, even in conflict situations. It didn't matter if we were loud. It didn't even matter if we were kind. We just talked it out and were friends again. Chuck came from the kindest family I had ever met and didn't show anger openly.

We came into our marriage with some unspoken rules. For me, it was okay to show anger openly, so when we had a disagreement and talked it out, even in anger, I thought we had succeeded. But Chuck thought we had failed. He usually kept quiet, which I assumed signaled his agreement with me. We had been married eleven years before he let me know that I ever did anything wrong.

Sometimes Chuck would get quiet, and I would ask him if anything was wrong.

"No, it's just my own little problem."

It was years before I knew that *I* was "his own little problem"!

Chuck and I both wanted the same thing for our marriage—peace. He walks away from conflict to keep the peace and I pursue it to make peace. I am expressive; he is nonexpressive. When we tried to talk things out, I knew that at a certain point Chuck would say, "You should just hear yourself!" and walk away. Each time we had a disagreement, I had to talk fast before Chuck used his exit line. You see, expressive people can talk and think faster than nonexpressive people. Chuck's walking away was a method he used to protect himself from me. After twenty-two years, Chuck couldn't hide his anger any longer. I was shocked! Here was a man who had seldom been angry with me (that I was aware of) now showing anger *toward me*. I didn't feel emotionally safe with him any longer. I never knew when he would suddenly and unexpectedly get angry. Things had changed.

About that time, we were invited to a Pro Athlete's Outreach Conference. We got to hear wonderful teachers like Gary Smalley, Larry Burkett, Tony Evans, Howard Hendricks, and many more. We also learned about a method of communicating called Quick Listening. We didn't try it for several years, but at some point we couldn't resolve our issues, so we decided to give it a try.

Quick Listening works like this. Whoever asks to have a Quick Listening session starts. We were taught that you give short feeling statements, and then the other person repeats back what was said. *But Chuck changed the rules*—he wanted to talk until he was through.

"But I can't remember everything you're getting wrong!" I told him.

"Take notes." He handed me a pen and paper. Chuck says nonexpressive people can't be interrupted every few words because they easily lose their train of thought. So I took notes, and when Chuck had finished, I paraphrased back to him everything he had said. I couldn't make comments or say he was wrong. I could only tell him what he had said, until I got it right. When he was satisfied that I had heard him, I told him how I saw the situation and he had to tell me what I had said, until he got it right. All this time we could not comment about whether the other person was right or wrong. We could only paraphrase what he or she had said. Then when we were through, we could talk freely back and forth.

Chuck says that by the end of that first time, he had become the debater William Buckley. He could talk with ease and without emotion, because for the first time he had all his thoughts out. I had never let Chuck finish a thought because I didn't think we should go on talking about something that according to me had never happened. The poor man had never finished a thought in thirty-three years!

The best thing I ever did for my marriage was to let Chuck speak until he was through, to let him complete a thought without interrupting him.

So simple, yet so hard.

But so worth it.

Isn't this a convicting story? Barb brings up such an important point. Each partner comes with his or her own "family rules" firmly attached. Barb can return to her birth family and be as expressive as she likes—that's familial behavior they've lived with all these years. But when she and Chuck hit a bump in the marital road, they needed to seek resolution in a new way. Thank goodness Barb was willing to give a "new way" a shot!

Most people aren't born with the inherent ability to listen, which is almost a lost art. Being a good listener is a learned trait. Begin today to listen to your husband. It's a courtesy he'll greatly appreciate.

Your husband has a point of view about things.
Can he freely and safely express it?

The Treasure of the Truce

No One Is Perfect Except Thee and Me,
but Sometimes I Wonder About Thee....

DONNA OTTO

The saying goes that "opposites attract—and then attack."
Nowhere is this seen more than in marriage. If, for example, your
personality is blunt, direct, and to the point, why is it that you seek
out and marry someone who just wants to have fun? This doesn't
seem to bother people who are dating, or they wouldn't get married.

I (Nancy) remember meeting and falling in love with my hus-
band, Ray. At the time I was living in Tokyo, Japan, working for
the American government, and he was in the Air Force. I marveled
that he would walk a mile down a muddy dirt road, rice paddies
on each side, just to see me—and never get even a speck of dirt on
his shoes or slacks. I loved that he said what he thought and that
when he said he'd be someplace at 7:00 P.M., he was not a millisec-
ond late.

After we married, though, it was quite surprising to me that he
never wanted to wear the same thing twice. It needed to be laun-
dered—and ironed as well! And why did he have to be so rude

(translation: he said what he thought), and what's the big deal if I ran a few minutes late?

Well, Donna Otto has come up with a wonderful solution to situations like these.

Why are smart people so dumb? Why do otherwise intelligent, well-adjusted, poised, and competent men and women lose all sense of control when they become husbands and wives and begin to disagree about such key topics as how to drive the car or turn off the lights at night? It's a great mystery. In my house, there is a very smart man and a very active woman who get themselves sideways with each other over the dumbest things. Sound familiar?

And these little disagreements can be like yeast, expanding in size, billowing up and out until they push us farther and farther apart. Soon our toes no longer touch in bed at night. All because of some silly disagreement over a small thing. And worst of all, I'm always right and he is always wrong, which makes the matter even more frustrating!

Maybe your house is filled with strong-willed people like mine is. God makes us gifted and strong for a purpose, but obviously the purpose is not to tear each other down. We become one flesh for a reason, and that reason is unity, not division. Yet God made us separate as well. Many books have been written about the differences between men and women and how these strange subspecies relate to one another (well, *he's* strange, anyway).

But one of the great testimonies of God's faithfulness is how He created men and women for intimacy with one another in marriage...intimacy on all levels and in a fashion that glorifies Him. When we put Him first, we open ourselves to enjoy intimacy in faith, in life, and in marriage.

Intense disagreements in marriage, which are part of life, can interfere with that spiritual and personal intimacy God intends. We are suddenly and thoroughly alone when we're cut off from fellowship with the Creator and with the partner He gave us. And alone is not good!

So after some years of marriage—and problems—David and I came to the conclusion that heated arguments that escalate into toe-chillers are stupid. We can do better than that, regardless of who is right or wrong. But how do you stop those rolling battles before they become deep canyons of separation?

We discovered the treasure of the truce.

We declare a truce! A truce is a halt to hostility. An immediate and complete cessation of whatever it is we are arguing about. We agree that in our marriage either party has the right to call a truce whenever he or she senses that a disagreement is starting to escalate. The other person must honor the truce.

Our truces have rules:

1. Anyone can call a truce at any time.
2. Each of us must immediately honor the truce, which means to stop talking and not try for some final cheap shot.
3. The truce lasts for three hours, during which time we cannot talk about the subject of dispute, or any other subject of dispute. There *will* be three hours of peace.
4. After the truce is over, we will talk about the disputed subject again. The issue does not go away. Only now, we are calm and usually embarrassed that things got a little out of control. The issue is usually quickly resolved and he apologizes. (Just kidding! Sometimes, I even apologize.)

Throughout history, truces have saved many a volatile situation. Diplomats use truces to stop hostilities, and so can you. It doesn't solve things, but it can save things. You still have to do the hard work of dealing with differences and disagreements, but you can do so without the salsa of emotion heating up your discussions.

Are things getting heated at your house? Agree to declare a truce! It's a smart answer to a dumb situation.

A few years ago Donna was a speaker at our annual women's retreat. One of the things she shared continues to guide us: "We all have goals, but so few of us are willing to take the little steps necessary to reach those goals." Donna has given us four little steps to reach a peaceful conclusion to the everyday disagreements all married couples face. The question is, will you take them?

Are you a peacemaker in your home?

Surely My Way Is the Right Way!

A Wife Who Is Willing to Learn—and Accommodate Her Husband—Is One of Life's Rarest Treasures

ESTHER M. OWCZAREK

*O*ne of the fascinations of having married children is watching them react to their spouse's way of doing things. This is especially true at major celebrations, such as Christmas. My (Nancy) daughter was shocked to learn that her new family had ham for Christmas instead of turkey. And because the family is large, they use Styrofoam plates to allow for rapid cleanup. Another daughter was horrified to see the way presents were unwrapped on Christmas morning. Her new family put each person's gifts in a separate section of the living room, and at the count of three, everyone quickly unwrapped their own stack of gifts, finishing in about a minute. How her husband must have suffered through our tradition of each person unwrapping one gift at a time, which took about two hours.

We can only imagine the joy Esther's new husband must've felt when Esther discovered within only eight months of marriage something that takes others years to learn…

Early in my married life, I grasped a truth that proved invaluable during that marriage, as well as in my present marriage (each of our previous mates passed away). I believe that God directed me to clearly see an important ingredient for living together in harmony.

The bit of insight I learned on a lovely spring day so many years ago is that *there is more than one right way to handle a situation.* When we walk down the marriage aisle, we generally come from two very different backgrounds, yet we often come into the marriage with the mind-set that there is only one way to accomplish a goal. And of course we always feel that our way is right!

My husband and I had been married about eight months when it came time to plant the garden. Garden seeds had been purchased with no problem, as each of us liked almost every kind of vegetable. The rototiller was in good working condition, rakes were clean, hoes had been sharpened, and we were ready to begin.

We opened the first row, planted the seed, closed the row, and stood smiling at each other with that smug satisfaction that said, "Our first garden will be a great success." Then it was time to mark the placement of our second row. I knew where the row should be: a precise eighteen inches from the first row. That was the distance my mother *always* placed her rows. My husband, on the other hand, insisted that the rows must be thirty-six inches apart. That was the distance between the rows in his parents' garden.

Our debate began. How could I get my husband to do it my way? I insisted that at thirty-six inches apart, we were not being good stewards of the soil. I thought we were wasting space. My husband tried to explain to me that a span of eighteen inches between the rows didn't allow room to walk, let alone to cultivate.

It was then that the Lord began to speak to me. Who was right? Who was wrong? Our garden plot had been small when I was growing up, so it was necessary to plant our rows close together to make use of every bit of space. My husband, on the other hand, grew up on a farm, where they tilled the garden with a tractor; thus, widely spaced rows were a necessity.

So who was right? Could it be possible we both were? After a time of discussion, I began to see where he was coming from. Given his background, his way of planting a garden was just as logical as mine. There was more than one right way.

Standing in the garden that afternoon, I began to see that if I wanted to live in harmony with my husband, I needed to be willing to look at each situation objectively and learn where my spouse was coming from and the reasons behind his thoughts and decisions. A simple "Honey, please explain your thoughts to me" has thwarted many an argument.

Harmonious living comes when we realize there may be several "right" ways. I found that I needed to be willing to look at all sides of an issue. This way of living takes practice though. We are selfish creatures by nature and want our own way at any cost. We are blinded into thinking our way is the only right way.

Thirty-three years have passed since God used a situation as simple as planting a garden to teach me an important truth. I am so thankful I chose to become a willing learner.

This must come as a shocking revelation to many. Esther has given us a major lesson in healthy relationship development. It involves selflessness, discernment, and real love to do things a new way. And the Lord is so good to us—if we don't learn a truth He puts before us, He'll give us the opportunity again…and again…and again. That's true, but wouldn't it be wonderful if we became quick learners? And wouldn't homes become havens if each of us made harmony in marriage our goal, as Esther did?

Esther is a living example of the Scripture, "Finally, all of you, live in harmony with one another; be sympathetic, love as brothers, be compassionate and humble."28 What a high calling! How long has it been since you genuinely expressed each of these emotions to your husband? Surely the woman who takes these words to heart, especially regarding her husband, lives the richest of lives.

Do you strive to make your home harmonious?

God's Tender Truths

Sometimes When We Slow Down,
We Hear Afresh from God

LYNDA DICK

When I (Connie) was a little girl and came down with any kind of illness, I could always count on one thing: As soon as Grandma got wind that I was sick, she'd be dropping by with some of her freshly made cornstarch pudding.

Her pudding could cure the worst of ills! It didn't matter if it was chicken pox, mumps, measles (yes, we had them "back then"!), or even a bad cold. Grandma's pudding made everything better.

Not long ago—in fact it was in the course of writing this book—I fell ill and spent a couple of days in bed. I asked my youngest daughter to call Mimi (my mother) and get Grandma's recipe. She and Wes mixed a batch of pudding that night, and it still made me feel better—even forty years later!

As I lay on the couch thinking about the many batches Grandma served up over the years, I realized that what made her pudding so special was her! Sure, the pudding was delicious, but what ministered to me more than anything else was knowing that Grandma cared.

Knowing that someone cares makes you feel better anytime—

especially when you're sick. And sometimes it takes an illness to slow us down and make us remember how wonderful our mates really are.

I never expected illness to have such an effect on my walk with God and my relationship with my husband. When I was forty, I needed an emergency hysterectomy. Good health and the ability to manage things fairly well had marked my life up to that point. Little did I realize, my health was about to decline and would severely affect being able to do things my way, and in my own strength.

I had a good relationship with God and with my husband, Ken. We were both believers when we met and had continued to walk with the Lord throughout our marriage. It sounds great, doesn't it? It really was, too, but soon God would be taking me through a spiritually deepening circumstance.

Prior to surgery, I came down with a kidney infection. This wiped me out physically and I was fatigued for a month. My Kenneth (as I often call him) was so sweet and helpful to me. He allowed me time to really rest and recharge. This, in turn, afforded me extra time with the Lord.

And I needed that time! We'd been married nineteen years, during which time I had taught high school until our first child was born, then began homeschooling when she was in second grade. We also had a preschooler and a nine-month-old. Life was busy and getting busier.

I was constantly in "zoom" mode and often found myself out of sorts with my husband and children. My main focus was on the kids and their schooling. Why do kids so often take priority over one's husband? Our marriage was solid, but

I really didn't devote much time to Ken.

During my kidney infection, I was able to spend larger chunks of time with God because I had to stay home and rest. During that time, God helped me come to the realization that I wasn't daily submitting myself to Him. He reminded me about walking by the Spirit moment by moment throughout each day. Then a few months later came the surgery and more resting time. I was able to get into God's Word every day and commit myself to Him.

Throughout all of this, Ken was so concerned for me. He cared for me, took me to my doctor appointments, and even shopped for me. He bought me a beautiful rose-colored robe for my hospital stay. He was helpful around our home, too. All of this deeply touched me. He shared with me and with others how this time of caring for me had caused him to fall in love with me all over again. I felt the same way.

Ken's love and God's prompting a new commitment to walk by the power of the Spirit caused our "solid" marriage to be woven throughout with a closeness and intimacy that had been lacking. Yes, it had been solid, but so is cement.

As I focused more on God, I was led to focus more on my husband, too. Now I was speaking to him sweetly instead of crabbily and building him up. My love for Ken blossomed. Through this time I renewed and refreshed my two great loves: my Lord and my husband.

God is awesome indeed! It is so like Him to bring joy and growth from a physically difficult time. I had fallen more deeply in love with Him *and* with my Kenneth.

Shortly after Lynda sent us her story, her husband read it. It caused him to think back to the days of Lynda's illness, and he sent us a brief e-mail and shared how he was changed during this time:

When Lynda got sick, it forced me to slow down and be more involved with her and at home. The thought of losing her was overwhelming to me. We cried and prayed together. I even broke down and cried in front of two hundred men the night I found out about her illness. When I stopped and spent time with her, I saw that all those wonderful characteristics that had made me fall in love with her were still there, but now with twenty years of maturation. Lynda has always been a servant by nature and she demonstrated that even more at this time.

Ken concluded his note:

The postscript to this story is that God used this same lesson to apply to my relationship with Him. I was studying Revelation at that time and was reading in chapter 2 about the church in Ephesus:

> *I know your deeds, your hard work and your perseverance. I know that you cannot tolerate wicked men, that you have tested those who claim to be apostles but are not, and have found them false. You have persevered and have endured hardships for my name, and have not grown weary. Yet I hold this against you: You have forsaken your first love. Remember the height from which you have fallen! Repent and do the things you did at first.[29]*

God pointed out that I was doing all the good things in my marriage, but needed to be awakened to the best things. God then pointed out, as only He can, that I had done the same to Him! It was time to remember, repent, and return. I have Lynda's name and the date of her surgery written next to this passage in my Bible so as never to forget my First Love and the gift He gave me in Lynda.

What a thrill to see the fruit of God's work in the lives of those willing to remember, repent, and return!

Have you forgotten your First Love?
Have you forgotten the love you once had for your husband?

Becoming a Good Sport

If You Want Sweet Music in Your Marriage,
Consider Singing His Song

RUTHIE THUNE

arrying is a bit like entering a university, imagining great times and parties and laughter…and then realizing that you actually have to go to class and study. When the stars that filled your eyes begin to fade and are replaced by bifocals, you realize that your beloved and his interests are quite different from you and your interests.

Some women try to convert their beloved to be more like them, but a prudent woman takes time to study her husband and adapt to him—even in matters of athletics!

The best thing I ever did for my marriage was to start reading the sports page. Let me explain.

My husband and I have differing interests. He is an athlete; I am a musician. When we were dating, I thought his interest in athletics was admirable and romantic. In addition to being interested in athletics, he was also very skilled. He was a star player on the basketball team, had done well at both baseball and soccer, and played football whenever he had the chance. I was delighted with his achievements.

But in the first year of marriage, I began to notice that on the days he played basketball after work, he was invariably late for dinner. He seemed to lose track of time. Sometimes they played beyond the scheduled time. I was disappointed that he didn't seem to have me in the back of his mind during his game and long to get home to me as quickly as possible. (Obviously, basic male/female differences had not registered!) I also began to notice that when there was a game on TV, his focus on our conversations bordered on comatose. I began to reconsider my view of his athletic interests and entertain the thought that his interest might pose a threat to my dominance of his time, attention, and loyalty.

I voiced this viewpoint to my brother one evening. He warned me against becoming a clutching, demanding wife rather than a wife who would release her husband to pursue his interests, confident that he would value her highly as his cheerleader. I was expecting a little more support for my developing viewpoint. I decided to go higher with my appeal and talked to the Lord about it in my prayer time. I was quite sure He wouldn't consider athletic interest to have eternal value.

A very interesting thought began to form in my heart as I prayed about the situation. I started to consider reading the sports page during the time I spent waiting for Bob's arrival so that I might communicate with him regarding the happenings in the sports world. At first I argued the logic of that thought. I knew next to nothing about sports! I would appear foolish! I was sure Bob would laugh out loud to hear me talk about athletic things. But for every objection I raised, the Spirit seemed to have an answer. This thought continued to impressed on my heart, and I knew I had come to a cross-roads: Would I obey what I felt the Lord was asking me to do and trust Him for the outcome, or would I continue to follow my feelings and control the situation myself?

I began to read the sports page. I had questions for Bob, and he answered them with delight and a curious enjoyment. As is always the case, God knew "the rest of the story" long before I did! He eventually blessed our home with two active boys who spent hours enjoying sports (good thing I was pre-pared!).

Reading the sports page began a practice that I believe is key for a wife: *Embrace the interests of your husband rather than viewing them as an enemy to be fought or a headache to be endured.* The result of this practice over the years is that your husband will grow to treasure you as the companion of his heart and the one who understands his soul. What could be a more appealing goal to the wife who longs to be needed? And what could be more nourishing to the husband who longs to be admired?

Ruthie is a close friend and we have tremendous admiration for her. Her husband is our senior pastor and has served several times on a panel in one of our classes. He and others have answered hundreds of questions about marriage, men, submission, sex, and anything else you can imagine.

Once, as a way of introducing each person on the panel, we called their wives ahead of time and asked each to share one thing she appreciated about her husband. Ruthie's reply was remarkable. She said that not once in thirty-four years of marriage had Bob ever intentionally hurt her feelings!

Can't you just picture women who are married to athletically inclined men dashing for the sports page each morning? Kind of funny, isn't it? And how wise it is for every woman to study her husband to see what interests him.

Do your husband's interests interest you?

Decisions! Decisions!

*Your Choices Can Either Trip
You Up or Move You Forward*

MARIE H. SMITH

*ave you ever noticed how yes and no decisions impact
your life—in big and small ways? As a kid, I (Connie) once said
yes to eating a three-pound bag of chocolate candy all at once and
paid for it with a huge stomachache. Several years later, as a
newlywed, I did the same thing! Wes was at work and we were
expecting company the following day. I had bought a big bag of
chocolates to keep the candy bowl supplied throughout the weekend. However, before Wes got home from work, the candy bowl
was empty and so was the bag of extra candy. And I discovered
that you still get stomachaches as adults when you decide to eat too
much candy in one sitting.*

*Decisions are a big deal! Your decisions determine whom you
marry, where you live, and what you believe. They're the foundation on which your life is built. And when you build a life, you
want to be certain that the foundation is solid.*

When I was six years old, my favorite dress was my "yes/no" dress. The soft dress had a net petticoat and a bright red sash. The white background was littered with yeses and nos, written in black cursive. I often wondered what each yes and no alluded to. I couldn't have imagined it then, but I had a lifetime of yes and no decisions ahead of me.

We make yes and no decisions one by one, with only the foresight the Lord grants at that time. In the realm of dating, as a relationship crystallizes into something more permanent, the future seems an ambiguous mirage on the horizon. Husband and wife are two strands woven together, strengthened by a third strand—their faith—to address the inevitable obstacles to come.

The early years of marriage are a time of discovery, challenge, and growth. There are different viewpoints and perspectives. There are mutual friends as well as friends who belong uniquely to one or the other.

Our marriage was no different. Our "culture" was that of academia and healthcare. Paul was in medicine, and I was a nurse. We were part of a vibrant fellowship of believers who stood by us at our wedding and in the ensuing years. The early months, while often consumed with work and adapting to married life, were thwarted by futile efforts to begin a family. Months marched by, punctuated by a miscarriage and additional failures to conceive. Eventually, after many more disappointments, we discovered we were pregnant with twins. The discovery on the ultrasound table brought tears of joyful anticipation. We were ecstatic! We shared our joy with everyone. The ever present nausea and vomiting were borne with anticipation and excitement.

Abruptly, we encountered a change. Our twins were born extremely prematurely. The year was 1982, and many of the medical advancements we have today weren't available to us then. The two sweet girls given to us by our Creator weathered incredible adversities. The following months in the ICU bound my husband and I ever tighter to our community at work and at church—and to one another. After what seemed like endless weeks and countless boxes of Kleenex, the girls came home. Their weights crested at ten pounds as they celebrated their first birthday, but soon it became obvious that due to her prematurity, one of the girls would be forever branded with cerebral palsy, blindness, and persistent seizures.

A decision needed to be made—my little yes/no dress was back in motion. Would I continue in my profession, which I so enjoyed, or stay home with our daughters? One would mean following a tenure track and editing nursing textbooks; the other would be saying yes to my daughters. One would be a walk of sight; the other a walk of faith. Paul supported the walk of faith. He also wanted to be able to have another child soon. Putting aside my fears of pregnancy and another premature delivery, as well as unremitting dreams of children with a variety of birth anomalies, I concurred.

The pregnancy progressed to a successful conclusion. We were blessed with a robust daughter—the antithesis of her still-underweight sisters. She was the picture of health and embraced life. The growth of our family and the end of Paul's residency converged. He had options for employment in the city we currently lived in. It was the birthplace of our children and the core of our support systems. It was the place where we began our marriage. It was the cradle of our fellowship. Yet Paul felt the call to return to his hometown. *The little dress swirled again.* I can remember listing the rationale of staying in our current environment. It was long on the side of staying. Among the reasons to return to Paul's hometown was the desire to be near his family. Would the answer be yes to move…or to stay?

To Paul, saying yes meant turning from the known to the unknown, from secure circumstances to insecure. The balance was tipped in his favor. With the move came new friends, a new language, and shared times with Paul's family. The satisfaction on Paul's face affirms that we are in the right place at the right time. I know without question that I'm in the right place, too.

At times, I still see the little girl twirling in front of the mirror in her yes/no dress. I know it will continue to swirl throughout my life. My heart's desire is to say yes to God and no to the world, but sometimes it's difficult! My prayer for myself, and for you as well, is that God will give us the grace to hear His voice and follow it.

Paul and Marie were good friends of ours (Connie) during that precious part of our lives when we were young, starting our families, and trying to get careers off the ground. We attended the same church in San Antonio, Texas, and we looked forward to seeing them every Sunday.

Marie once gave me a poignant picture of what "bittersweet" looks like. The occasion was their twins' fourth birthday. It had been a bittersweet kind of day. "We bought them both a set of wheels," she explained. "It's just that one set belonged to a shiny new bicycle and the other set belonged to a pediatric wheelchair." The healthy twin was ready to ride a bike; the twin with cerebral palsy had outgrown the stroller and now needed a wheelchair. Two modes of transportation for two very different little girls, each one knitted together in Marie's womb by God Himself.

Today the twin who received the bicycle is pedaling all over Vanderbilt University. Their third daughter, who hit life running, continues at that pace at the University of Virginia. They have a teenage son in high school who looks just like his dad. And what of their adored twin daughter who struggled so mightily on this earth? She now rests in the arms of her heavenly Father.

Marie has faced tragedy that few of us will ever know. Yet her faith remains strong. The decision she made years ago to know God intimately has given her comfort through even the darkest situations. She has come to know Jesus as Savior, Lord, Provider, Protector, Comforter, and Friend. She rests in the knowledge that when you say yes to God, you can trust Him with the outcome.

Are you in the habit of saying yes to
God and trusting Him for the outcome?

A Man of Integrity

...Is to Be Treasured

CHRISTINE PALMER BURKETT

igh on a husband's list of needs is something central to a man's sense of well-being and self-worth: respect. With it he can press on amid defeat and climb the highest marital mountain.

Many women feel that their husbands must earn their respect. This is simply not true! We are to respect our husbands simply because God said so. His Word even tells us what this looks like: "Let the wife see that she respects and reverences her husband [that she notices him, regards him, honors him, prefers him, venerates, and esteems him; and that she defers to him, praises him, and loves and admires him exceedingly]."[30] Even if a woman has stopped respecting her husband's behavior, she must respect his title; otherwise she undermines the foundation of her home.

My (Nancy) sister, Christine, learned this lesson early in her marriage through a series of on-the-job encounters with her husband's integrity. I have seen her model what God taught her. Spending a week at their home is like attending an advanced course in how to respect and love one's husband.

I find Carl delightful. He is totally winsome in his honesty. He is completely free of guile, as honest as a child. I have come to find this quality charming.

But it wasn't always so.

Recently I was visiting my dad in Virginia, while my husband remained home in Texas. Carl called to tell me that a couple had invited him over the night before for dinner. He went on to tell me that she made the best spaghetti he'd ever tasted and that they gave him the leftovers, which he was going to eat that night. I asked him if it was as good as my spaghetti, and he said, without hesitation, "It's much better!" He was totally oblivious to having just expressed an opinion—which most husbands know is taboo! I have seen husbands' heads snap up in disbelief when Carl has said similar things in their presence. Hushes fall upon conversations, and every eye turns toward me to see how I'll react. My reactions today are much different than in the past.

In our early years, I felt that I had to watch Carl closely so he wouldn't offend anyone. You see, I'm Mrs. Tactful. I bend over backward trying not to offend anyone, as my best friend Mo well knows. Our conversations usually go something like this:

"Christine, would you like to go to see a play with me tomorrow evening? Tony will be out of town, so I have an extra ticket."

"Oh, Mo, that sounds like so much fun. I always have the best time with you. But I *do* have to work tomorrow and get up early. But the play sounds wonderful; how sweet of you to think of me."

Mo, who has broken my code (what my sister and I have

dubbed as "sister talk"), says simply, "Are you coming or not? Yes or no!"

After several more word flurries, I'll admit that I won't be going. Carl would have said "No thanks" immediately.

In my early days with Carl, I was determined that he would learn this marvelous art of tactfulness. In my mind he was blunt and insensitive. I soon had a great training opportunity, which took a huge wrong turn and made me appear very foolish. We were climbing the stairs to a friend's apartment for a get-together, when I saw a man with a hook for a hand on the landing. Immediately I thought, *DANGER! Carl cannot be trusted near this man!* Perhaps if I prepared him with a lesson in sensitivity, nothing tactless would happen. So I whispered, "Darling, please don't ask that man with the hook how he lost his hand."

"What are you talking about?"

"Well, you sometimes just say what comes into your head, but I don't want you to embarrass the man, okay?"

Later we were conversing with this man, and Carl, after some pleasant small talk, had lulled me into a false sense of security. He suddenly blurted out, "My wife told me not to ask you this, but I'm going to ask anyway. How did you lose your hand?" The man looked at me, then at Carl, and began with obvious relief to share the circumstances surrounding one of the most significant events in his life. I was mortified! I later wondered how many other significant events in people's lives we had missed out on because I thought my "tactfulness" was better.

As Carl and this man talked about his hook hand, I was able for the first time to see Carl's directness for what it was: a gift. He's not afraid to talk about the "elephant in the room" that everyone else pretends not to notice. In doing so, he puts people at ease.

Perhaps Carl is on to something. Perhaps I'm not as right as I thought…and perhaps he's not as wrong, I mused.

I began to attend a study at my church because I wanted to be a wife God's way. As I dedicated myself to being transformed by the renewing of my mind,[31] I discovered that God was very interested in my marriage. The verse that began changing me was, "Let the wife see that she respects and reverences her husband."[32] Could it be that my attitude toward my husband was all wrong? This verse collided with my long-held belief that a man has to earn his wife's respect. I was dumbfounded. *Anyone who knows anything about psychology can tell you that respect must be earned,* I argued. *What? This is my job? I have to be the initiator of respect?*

But God's Word was clear. I was to respect my husband because God said to. I couldn't believe I had taken the world's value system and mistaken it for truth. How could I fix what my faulty belief system had damaged? I loved my husband, but he had traits that I found irritating. I was constantly in the process of compiling an inner list of things that were wrong with Carl. This attitude had undermined my respect for him, which caused me to grumble about him in my heart. I confessed this and asked God to help me learn what He meant by the verse and how to obey it. Soon afterward, I picked up a book about the role of a Christian wife. I opened by chance to a chapter on how to restore respect for one's husband.

The Counselor was about to counsel me. The thrust of the message was that a wife should make a list of ten qualities she admires about her husband. She should continually thank God for each of these traits for thirty days.

I decided to give it a try. I prayerfully concentrated on

Carl's good qualities and soon had a list of things I truly respected about him. I began to thank the Lord every night for each good quality. Before long, I knew the list by heart, and it was taking the place of that ugly list I had earlier compiled.

One day, shortly after I had begun my prayers of thanksgiving, Carl came home from the grocery store, flushed. He told me that a young man had opened his car door and slammed it into an elderly woman's door. When the woman said something, the man cursed at her. Carl went up to the man, asking what he thought his mother would think of such behavior, and inquired if his mother raised him to be so disrespectful to an older woman. The young man stood there shamefaced.

I asked how big the man was. Carl wanted to know what that had to do with anything. I then suggested that the man could have attacked him and knocked him down. Carl told me he would have bitten his ankle. (How can anyone not find my husband charming?) I continued, telling him he could get hurt in situations like that. I'll never forget his reply:

"Our country is going downhill because everybody is afraid to get involved or step up when they see something wrong happen. I am not going to look the other way and let bad things go unchallenged. I am going to take a stand."

At that moment, I saw Carl for who he is—a man of rare courage and principle. And I felt proud. And I felt respect. My husband is a man of integrity.

God chose that moment to show Christine that her former list of Carl's faults was not accurate. She had simply mislabeled his very best qualities—the things she now cherishes most. And of all things, the most distinguishing trait of Carl's that she had labeled blunt, tactless, and insensitive is really the hallmark of godly character: integrity!

It's a beautiful thing to be sensitive to the promptings of the Holy Spirit. Way to go, dear sister!

Will you begin today to write a list of ten qualities you admire about your husband?

New York City Meets Dog Patch, USA

Your Relationship with Your In-Laws Is a Good Barometer of the Condition of Your Own Heart

DEANNIE PRICE

Isn't it interesting to explore your family trees? Just last week, I (Nancy) received a document from my father's side of the family. My cousin had gone to great lengths to uncover the history of our family. The facts, coupled with anecdotes of various family members, are sprinkled with humor, heroics, and some things that might raise an eyebrow. It's one thing to interact with a document and quite another to interact with a person, especially a testy one!

Let's face it, we sometimes think that not only did our beloved come from Mars; his family of origin sprang up on Pluto.

Young love is blind to so much. I was only eighteen when I married and was completely in the dark about many things. For example, I believed that my wonderful Prince Charming and I would float off into our new future together...just the two of us…*alone*. After all, wasn't that the way it happened in the movies?

I didn't realize that marriage is sort of a package deal. Along with my prince came an entire family—his family! And now they were *my* family, too. I quickly discovered that they weren't just like my prince. In fact, they weren't *anything* like him. There was a real assortment of personalities, habits, values, and opinions. Bob once said that getting our two families together was just like combining New York City and Dog Patch, USA.

The most prominent of these new family members was my mother-in-law. Before saying "I do," I hadn't spent even a minute thinking about how she and I would relate with each other. As we became acquainted, I knew that if I were to seek out a warm and caring relationship with an older woman, I wouldn't pick her. I was sure we had nothing in common, and she probably felt the same way about me.

She used "colorful" language—I heard words from her that my mother had sheltered me from my entire life. She had strong opinions and stated them with a force that was way beyond my comfort level. She enjoyed sharing her opinions in public places such as at a store, or among a crowd of people. She was a smoker; I choked on smoke. But she wasn't just a smoker; she was a smoker with an attitude. She was stubborn. She believed that her way of doing things was the best way, and compromise seemed a foreign concept to her. She was a no-frills woman who believed that "good enough to get by" should be life's standard and that being on time was the highest form of godliness. My approach to life was that you could never have too many frills, and that every moment should be made into a special one. This takes time, of course, so living with this sort of zest could occasionally cause punctuality to fall by the wayside.

One of the biggest roadblocks was our difference of opinion about religion. Whenever Bob and I attempted to share our faith with his parents, we were met with resistance. This aspect of our relationship became more strained over time, so we avoided it.

As the years rolled by, Bob's mom and I developed a certain level of acceptance toward one another. I dutifully visited Bob's parents and welcomed them when they visited us. But I held an unspoken opinion that my family was better, and I much preferred their company.

Then, as I was meditating on some of the "love" verses in the Bible, God began to do a work in my heart. I began to comprehend His unconditional love for me. If God really loved me unconditionally, then I wanted Him to help me learn to love others that way. I prayed that He would help me love my mother-in-law like He loved her. I confessed to Him that on my own I couldn't, and that He would have to help me. I asked Him to help me see her as He saw her.

God began to change things. The first thing He changed was *me*. He softened my heart and helped me see my mother-in-law's vulnerabilities and needs. Slowly, I began to accept her just as she was. He then checked my silent judgments of her. As I submitted to Him, *He began to love her through me.*

Love is a funny thing. When you offer an environment of loving acceptance, the person usually begins to love you back. And she did. During the last few years of her life, my mother-in-law would boastfully tell people that I was the daughter she never had.

At age seventy-nine she suffered a massive stroke and wasn't expected to live through the night. We grieved because she had never made the decision to surrender to Christ. But God still had plans for her life. She survived and after nearly three months in the hospital was able to go home. I cared for her as she got settled and learned new routines to help her adapt. During that time, God allowed me to witness a miracle.

One day she initiated a spiritual conversation, and I was able to help her see her need for a Savior. It was so precious to witness her rebirth, and with halting, stroke-damaged speech she invited Christ into her life. We shared tears of joy as we finished the prayer. She said that she felt she needed to say the prayer again because God might not have understood her. I told her that God understood her heart, and that was all that mattered.

My mother-in-law lived for three more years. She began to read the Word and got involved in a Bible study. Her attitude softened, and she learned how to forgive. Some things didn't change much, though. She continued to be a smoker with an attitude! And she tried to leave her colorful language behind and soften her opinions, but seventy-nine-year-old habits are hard to break.

I believe that I unknowingly caused a tug-of-war for Bob in the early years of our marriage. I was silently encouraging him to choose my family over his. After all, who wouldn't choose New York City? I felt pleased when he would tell me that he preferred being with my family. But acceptance of our roots and knowing that God uses everything in our life to shape us is so important.

My changed attitude toward Bob's mom was a wonderful tonic for our marriage. It allowed Bob to relax and love and enjoy his parents just as they were, without any expectations that they would change to meet someone else's standards. And the special gift that gave our marriage is twofold: We are able to share some very special memories of his parents, and more important, we rejoice in knowing that we'll be reunited with them in heaven one day.

Deannie's story is one we can all relate to. She made a conscious decision, after discovering what true love looks like, to love unconditionally. Jesus discusses love again and again. One riveting point He makes is, "If you only love the lovable, do you expect a pat on the back? Run of the mill sinners do that. Don't pick on people, jump on their failures, and criticize their faults, unless, of course, you want the same kind of treatment. Give away your life. You'll find life given back, but not merely given back; given back with bonus and blessing. Giving, not getting, is the way. Generosity begets generosity."[33]

Generosity begets generosity. Isn't that the way you want to live?

Whom do you need to love more generously?

section five

Refined
by Fire

*Laugh, cry, and rejoice as you read how
these women faced some of life's most
difficult challenges. It seems that God
often does His deepest work in the midst
of sorrow, grief, betrayal, and loss.
Journey with these women as they share their
stories, and be inspired and encouraged by the
fresh truths each learned about God.*

When Another Man Enters the Picture

To Love Your Husband Is to Faithfully Guard Your Heart

ANONYMOUS

Ever started out going one place…only to end up somewhere else? We know of one couple that was taking a summer vacation through Wyoming and Montana. The husband drifted off to sleep when the wife was behind the wheel, and when he woke up they were in Idaho! His wife had missed an exit and thus landed them in a place they never intended to visit!

Sometimes this can happen in a marriage as well. Someone "drifts" off briefly, and the couple finds themselves in a place they never intended to be. Hear firsthand what can happen if you linger a little too long in a place you shouldn't be. And hear as well how God can create beauty from even the ugliest of situations.

I remember it like it was yesterday. It was a beautiful fall day, when my son was just a young boy. I had been pushing him on the swing in the backyard of our new home. We had just celebrated our fourteenth anniversary and were blessed with three children. Our marriage was strong and life couldn't be better. As my son played in the sandbox, I sat and thought about how happy I was. I was so happy it almost made me afraid that something bad might happen and destroy that happiness. At the time I was thinking of the death of a loved one. Little did I realize, the choices I would make in the next year could result in the death of my marriage.

One great thing about our new home was the neighbors. We became especially close to one family—hitting it off right from the start. As the weeks went by, the guys would help each other on various projects. I especially loved it when our neighbor came over to help with chores at the house. He was "repair smart" and was such a help. Plus, he was so much fun to have around. He often teased the kids and me, and we shared a sense of camaraderie. I always made sure I touched up my makeup if I knew ahead of time that he was coming.

After a year or so, this man started calling to talk to my husband during the middle of the day. Of course he was at work, but instead of calling there, he would talk to me. We would chat for long periods and I looked forward to his calls. After a few weeks, I finally asked him why he called in the middle of the day. I'll never forget his reply: "I really like talking to you…maybe a little too much." Those words began an affair faster than a person can flush a toilet. And the comparison, by the way, is appropriate.

What began in February lasted through June, with neither party experiencing any guilt. We lied without a second thought. It's amazing how difficult it becomes to even see the truth, let alone tell it. We began talking about leaving our spouses. It makes me sick to admit this, but I began to think that the only way I would ever really be happy was to be with him.

Then something happened. He attended a Christian conference for men and came back from the weekend determined to stay with his wife and children. I was devastated. My world seemed to cave in at that point. I had never felt so alone.

I remember sitting in church week after week praying that God would send someone to help me. I knew I had messed up my life, but I felt I had nowhere to turn. Who would want to help me after all I'd done? Whom could I trust with this awful secret? The feeling of aloneness was overwhelming. *I wanted to die.*

I'd been a Christian for almost twenty years. I knew that what I had been doing was wrong, but I felt powerless to get out of it. I was so confused. I really didn't want to give up this other man. I wanted what I wanted. Surely I had a "right" to happiness. I knew God loved me and understood my struggle. And I knew He understood my "need" to be happy.

Of course He understood all of this! And He knew, without question, that what I needed was not the love of another man. What I needed was discipline and wisdom to go His way, not my own.

After months of turmoil, I finally accepted the fact that I could not have this other man. I knew I needed to surrender my "right" to have my way and accept God's plan for me. I still wrestled with my emotions, but I knew I had to start by asking God to forgive me. I asked Him to show me what to do to get over this man. He impressed on my heart that I needed to tell my husband the truth. I didn't know how he would respond, but I knew I had to do it. It was our only hope.

There were lots of ups and downs emotionally for both of us, but his commitment to our marriage carried us through.

Even though I hadn't been faithful, he chose to be. He chose to forgive me even if he didn't feel like it. I thank God that my husband was committed to Him, for it was this commitment that enabled my husband to carry out his commitment to me, even in the midst of betrayal and pain.

We began seeing a Christian counselor. His initial advice for us was to move away. This seemed like such a *serious* thing to do. Well, it *was* serious! To think otherwise would be foolish. The counselor shared that couples who move after going through something like this learn once again to depend on each other and to rebuild their friendship. The ones that don't move have a much more difficult time.

Amazingly enough, just days later a friend called my husband regarding a job opportunity, which we pursued. As hard as it was to uproot and start over, it was the right choice for us. We were forced to depend on each other and to communicate and reconnect. I needed him like never before. We were miles from home and he was my only friend. We got involved in a church and over time healing began.

There are no quick and easy recovery methods to any addiction. The attachment I formed to this other man was a very powerful emotional addiction. You have to treat extramarital affairs—both physical and emotional—as an addiction. They may not be chemical in nature, but there is an invisible bond that forms between the two people involved. Those invisible bonds are formed very simply: one poor decision, one lie at a time. As the relationship continues, the bond becomes stronger and stronger. You feel far more connected with this person than with your own spouse. The fact that it's shrouded in deceit matters little. Eventually these bonds become so powerful that you're willing to do almost anything in order for them to continue.

At any point in time, however, you can stop the process by simply choosing to tell the truth. That's what I did when I finally told my husband. The truth breaks the powerful hold of deceit. Almost instantly, I felt some of the bonds with the other man begin to weaken. It didn't immediately fix everything, but like the layers of an onion, slowly the hard crusty outer layers of my heart came off, and I was freed.

It's been several years now since that beautiful fall day outside with my son. Our marriage is closer than it has ever been. We're happy and have been able to help others in similar situations.

Below are some basic principles I learned through this ordeal:

- Never tell yourself that it can't happen to you—it can. Saying it can't happen gives a false sense of security and may cause you to place yourself in situations you shouldn't be in.
- Thank God for your spouse daily. Ask God to help you love him.
- Don't compare. Comparison and dissatisfaction are often the beginnings of a dark, downward spiral.
- If you have romantic feelings for someone else, terminate contact immediately. Tell your spouse. If you don't feel you can, tell a trusted friend. Adultery starts in the heart. If you're having recurring thoughts about another man, including imaginary conversations, trying to look good when you see him, or trying to manipulate circumstances to run into him, this is adultery of the heart. Call it what it is: a sin.
- Don't have lengthy conversations with another man, either in person or on the phone. Never be in a room

alone with him. Don't share "secrets" or anything else you wouldn't share if your spouse were listening.

- Never discuss your spouse or your unhappiness in your marriage with this person. To do so is like firing a cannonball straight through your spouse's heart, and the ensuing pain can be nearly unbearable. Your spouse will feel betrayed, and his trust will be severely wounded. Also, doing this sets the other man up as a "knight in shining armor," who feels the need to rescue the damsel in distress.
- Refuse to allow a person of the opposite sex to discuss their marital problems with you. *Immediately* refer them to a friend or counselor.
- *Never* tell another man that you are attracted to him.
- Make holiness, rather than happiness, your goal. You might be surprised at how the former often leads to the latter.
- Stay in God's Word! Pray alone and as a couple. If this is uncomfortable, pray together silently.
- Don't expect your spouse to meet your deepest needs. There are things only God can do for us.
- Realize that the hurt you caused your spouse will not go away quickly. When a third party gets involved in a marriage, it can take a long time for the pieces to be put back together. Don't think, *Why can't you just get over this? It's over.* It won't be over for your spouse for a very long time. Shattered trust doesn't put itself together overnight.
- Stop thinking that there couldn't be any pain out there worse than the pain you feel in your marriage. There is. And you'll quickly find that out if you make wrong decisions during this time of crisis.

- Never again look at the person with whom you were involved as "neutral" or "nice." He is about as neutral and nice as a loaded and aimed machine gun. Realize that he can't be trusted with the well-being of you or your family.
- Be willing to go all-out in loving your spouse day after day after day—for the rest of your life. As one counselor said, "You're the one who drove this truck off the road; you need to take responsibility for getting it back on the road."

I often lie awake at night and think about my life. I'm thankful for my husband and family and for God's protection even when I was disobedient. Things could have been so different. The lives of those I love most could have been shattered. I deserved punishment, and yet I received mercy and a new start.

I feel many things…joy, relief, contentment, amazement.

Most of all, I feel forever grateful. Grateful and forgiven.

If you've taken a wrong turn in your marriage and are currently in a place you shouldn't be, run to God and ask Him to help you get out. The very hearts and souls of the ones you love most deeply are on the line.

Extricating yourself from such a place isn't easy or fun. In fact, it can be one of the hardest things you'll ever do—but it will also be one of the best decisions you'll ever make. Refuse to listen to those voices in your mind telling you that you deserve a little excitement and intrigue.

Third parties should never be allowed into a marriage, but if they have been, it is important for the offended spouse to forgive both the spouse and the third party involved. If he doesn't, he will develop a cold, bitter heart and remain in bondage. This can wreck a life as much or more than the original offense. Forgiveness is vital for the health of all involved.

The best defense against an affair is to continually invest in your marriage. Don't put it on the back burner, as so many couples do. Invest in it daily!

Can you say to your spouse at day's end,
"I have been faithful to you today with my words,
my actions, and my thoughts"?
If not, what do you need to do to change?

When You've Been Betrayed

Forgiving in the Most Difficult Situations

DEBRA CRAFT

The last thing a woman expects to be part of her love story is betrayal. How grievous, how wounding… The devastation this young bride must have experienced is unimaginable. But as you'll soon see, she didn't allow this tragedy to define her.

Adultery is a very grave matter. Marriage is sacred, and God has ordained that it mysteriously unites a couple so that they become one. Jesus, when questioned about this, said, "Anyone who divorces…except for marital unfaithfulness, and marries…commits adultery."[34]

But forgiveness is never optional. Our friend Debra didn't necessarily have to reunite with her husband, but she did need to forgive him, as hard as that must've been in the midst of betrayal.

John and I were crazy about each other. We married at the tender age of eighteen. I loved everything about being married—in a sense, it defined who I was.

Both John and I were raised in Christian homes but had strayed from a relationship with God. Going to church was the last thing on our minds. Partying and doing things we shouldn't took priority. There was always a check in my spirit, but we were allowing worldly influences to play a bigger and bigger part in our lives. Over time, a gap the size of the Grand Canyon had developed in our relationship with each other and with the Lord. It was subtle; it didn't happen overnight. We were completely unaware of the danger that was lurking, waiting to pounce on a naive, unsuspecting young couple.

Another woman! Amazingly, she would be the tool God used to teach me forgiveness. At the time, I didn't see forgiveness as an option in restoring my relationship with my husband. The word was foreign to me, really.

Lord, I would cry, *how could You let this happen?* I saw the affair as a total affront to my very character and who I was as a woman. The words *You've been betrayed!* rang in my mind over and over again. *Betrayed by your husband* and *by your God!* I felt devastated on both counts.

John and I separated. During the months that followed, I learned that when your spirit is damaged, it is the hardest hurt to overcome. I also learned that God hadn't betrayed me—I'd betrayed Him. I had left my first love. We both had.

As John and I worked through the affair, God continually reminded me of promises I had made as a wife. *Well, okay, Lord, I've kept my promises—what about John?*

"I'm only interested in *your* promise. You remember the one about 'for better or worse' and 'till death do you part'?"

Sure, I remembered those words, but that would mean I had to forgive. Why should I forgive when he'd had the affair?

"Why? Because I've forgiven you!" God's words pierced my heart.

I had to forgive! I had no choice. For personal and marital restoration to take place, I needed to forgive. It was difficult, but I've found that forgiveness is the best thing I can do for my marriage. If love is the bond that holds a marriage together, then forgiveness is the glue.

How did I forgive? It was a day-by-day decision—a choice I made every day. Along the way, I learned a number of lessons:

1. How you live your life is your choice, your decision.
2. Allowing yourself to become consumed with unforgiving- ness hurts everyone. It is a spiritual sickness.
3. Choosing to forgive each day causes a deep, inner healing that is unexplainable.
4. You can refuse Satan's attempts to remind you of the past. If he can keep you dwelling on it, you get stuck and don't move on. Each time the thought of it comes up, think on other things.

God says, "For if you forgive men when they sin against you, your heavenly Father will also forgive you. But if you do not forgive men their sins, your Father will not forgive your sins."[35] Our heavenly Father must be busy keeping up with my sins. I asked God to forgive me and am so thankful that when I did, He forgave me completely. I know there are no reruns in His mind about me.

John and I have been married for thirty-one years. The best thing I ever did for my marriage? I put into practice the principle of forgiveness. When I did, I learned what love is really all about.

Right now, Debra and John are walking through a time that is testing their faith and causing them to cling to one another and to God especially tightly. John has been diagnosed with two types of cancer and is currently undergoing treatment for both.

How thankful they must be that their love for each other kept them from buying into the world's concept of commitment. Being together and loving each other now means so much more than ever before because of the choice they made early in their marriage to forgive. This is living with eternity in mind!

Are you living with eternity in mind?

"Daddy, What's Divorce?"

When Dad Walks out, a Daughter
Wonders If She Can Ever Trust a Man Again

JULIE BRESTIN

*L*ittle girls' hearts and dreams can be deeply damaged by the broken promises of their parents. Trust gives way to fear. Love seems to have "what ifs" and "supposes" attached to it. And when they grow up to be big girls and begin making decisions that involve commitment, the specter of doubt brings the past far too brilliantly into the present. Daughters wounded by divorce become women who cautiously guard their hearts. They have an inordinate sense of mistrust, even when they fall head over heels in love with the very one who is the answer to their prayers.

I was just a little girl, jumping on the bed at the hotel. I was *so* excited. My parents were taking my brothers and me to Disneyland that day. On the television, a show called *Divorce Court* came on, and I asked, "Daddy, what's divorce?"

"It's when people decide they don't want to be married anymore," he answered.

I stopped jumping, fear stilling my excitement. "Will that ever happen to you and Mommy?"

"No, honey."

Two years later, Dad walked out our front door, suitcase in hand. Like every child, I thought my parents were perfect. They wouldn't fail, wouldn't break their word, wouldn't let me down. Yet that day the rock beneath my feet crumbled. The rock beneath my mom's feet crumbled, too. I watched her go into a severe depression. She became thin and withdrawn, losing confidence in her worth.

When I was a teenager, I saw this whole scene repeated when my grandfather walked out on my grandmother. Was there anyone who would never betray me, never fail me, and never desert me? Would this same scenario, which had devastated my mother and grandmother, one day happen to me? I decided I couldn't trust anyone. This left me in a hopeless state, but God, in His mercy, reached out to me during that vulnerable time.

I went to visit my Aunt Jo, and she began talking to me about Jesus, the One who would never leave me. She told me that even the best people would let me down, because every person has feet of clay. But Jesus was without sin—He was the Rock that would never crumble beneath my feet. I could trust Him. I learned that I could love people, I could marry and give my love to a husband, but my security needed to be in Jesus—and not in any person, no matter how dear. Even the kindest people cannot promise that they will never fail you. I must find my security in Christ alone. I believe that the best thing I have ever done for my marriage, and can continue to do, is to put my trust in Jesus and not in my husband. I can run to Jesus for His wisdom and His help, and I can love people but also give them the freedom to fail, for I have One who never will.

God has been incredibly faithful to me. Shortly after I put my trust in Christ, I prayed for godly friendships and that God would give me a husband from a strong Christian home. I devoured the Scriptures, seeking to know right from wrong. One night at a Fellowship of Christian Athletes gathering, I gave a brief talk on the negative effects of rock and roll. I was just fifteen and perhaps a bit black-and-white in my thinking, but I shared from my heart.

All the girls knew John Brestin, a good-looking football player. He was seventeen, and that night I noticed him sitting between two girls. Unbeknownst to me, John had recently come out of a rebellious time in his life, had recommitted his life to Christ, and had prayed for a godly girl. One of the negative influences in his life had been rock and roll music. He listened to me intently and after the meeting he came over and talked to me. I was pretty excited by his attention.

A few months later my friend Jill had a going-away party for me because I was going to spend my junior year of high school as an exchange student in Mexico. John was there, and afterward we got into an animated discussion about spiritual things and talked late into the night. It was such an amazing experience for me to see how clearly God was answering my prayer for friends who could mentor me—and to find this young man who talked so passionately about Jesus. In John I saw a man who had great wisdom regarding the truth of God, a man who knew the difference between right and wrong.

I was humbled by God's mercy, and I was also falling in love. I'll never forget our parting the next day. We were stand-

ing in the driveway, saying good-bye, when he leaned down
and gave me a quick kiss on the cheek. He said, "I'll write
you." Then he drove off in his car. As he neared the corner, he
rolled down his window and yelled, "*I'm crazy about you!*"

I floated into the house. How I hoped he would be true
to his word and write, but I knew I shouldn't count on it
because people don't always keep their promises. But John *did*
write, almost every day for a year. We continued to develop
our relationship through letters. I believe that God, again in
His mercy and faithfulness, was helping us get to know each
other without any temptation of physical involvement.

Three and a half years later, we knew each other very
well, and by God's grace and a lot of Scripture memory and
accountability, we were still physically pure. We were counseling one summer at a Christian camp when John surprised
me with a most romantic proposal.

During our courtship, and in our twelve years of marriage, we have always known that our relationship could only
be strong and lasting if it was centered on Jesus. It was just as
vital to realize that each of us was capable of failure. This led
to an incredibly healthy relationship, in which John and I had
the freedom to fail and would forgive each other, love each
other, and realize that our marriage did not depend on our
infallibility, but on our infallible God. We asked God to help
us be true, and to strengthen us. One thing He showed us
was the importance of honoring one another and never
speaking negatively about one another to others. He also
showed us that it was important never to threaten or even
entertain the idea of divorce. What security this has provided!
And it's one of the ways God is helping me break free of the
sin cycle that was so hurtful to my parents and grandparents.

John once took me to a nearby shop and asked me to

pick out a silver ring. We'd just had an argument. As he placed the ring on my finger, he said, "This is to remember that we will always work it out. I will always take care of our family and our marriage."

I have a faithful God in whom I can place my trust. This is such a peaceful and freeing place to be! There's no better place!

Julie is a dear friend of ours, and the family she married into offered her a built-in mentor—Dee Brestin, a gifted speaker and the author of numerous books on relationships. Because Julie knows she has a God who is faithful, she has ceased struggling against life's uncertainties.

If you have children—whether they are tiny or grown—pray for them. Pray that God will bless them with godly spouses one day. One young man we know broke up with a woman he was considering marrying because he knew his mother had prayed for years for his spouse and he felt in his heart she wasn't the right one. A few years later, he knew without doubt that he'd met "her." His mother's prayers had sensitized in him the desire for a godly spouse. If your children are already married, pray for their spouses. Love them as Christ would love them.

In whom have you placed your trust?

When Your World Is Turned Upside Down

*A Chilling Phone Call Could Be the Very
Thing That Brings You Closer to God*

PATTI RHEA

*Ever had the phone ring in the middle of the night? Your
stomach immediately does a flip, and your mind races through an
amazing number of possibilities in mere seconds: Has something
happened to a family member? Has there been an accident? Are all
the kids tucked safely into bed? Maybe you even utter a quick prayer
as you grope for the phone:* Please, God, let everything be okay.

*More often than not, the calls turn out to be either pranks or
wrong numbers. But sometimes the calls are serious, and when
they are, life is never the same again.*

*Patti received such a call, and her world was turned upside
down. Or, as you'll see, right side up. Until then she hadn't realized
just how upside down her life had become.*

I said "I do" three weeks after I turned twenty-eight. My husband, Pete, was several months away from his thirtieth
birthday on that blessed September day. We both knew the

sacredness of taking our wedding vows before a holy God. Divorce would never be an option.

Pete and I came into marriage with our eyes wide open. We had observed unhealthy patterns in our circle of acquaintances. In each case, expectations went unmet, leading to deep hurts and wounds. We knew we wanted a different path. We wanted Jesus to be the center of our marriage. I decided that I wouldn't depend on Pete to fulfill the needs that only the Lord could fill. Yet little did I realize how that very "spiritual" attitude would lead to a spirit of pride later....

I had heard that many people struggle in their first year of marriage, but Pete and I didn't. It was terrific. We enjoyed each other's company and stayed in the Word and in fellowship with other believers.

During our second year of marriage, we started a family. For the next several years we still had what I considered to be a good marriage. Looking back, I can see how very often I let the "tyranny of the urgent" take priority over what was truly important. I found myself being all too busy with the everyday things of life. Children, school, my job, and the "things of the world" had forced the Lord onto the back burner. Many times I was "too tired" not only for the Lord, but also for fulfilling my husband's needs. I sensed that Pete was becoming aloof and somewhat distant.

Then my world was turned upside down—or, as the truth became known, right side up. In February of 1995, at the age of forty-three, I went to the doctor for a mammogram. The next afternoon I received that dreaded call from my doctor telling me that I needed to have a biopsy. I went to a breast cancer specialist for a second opinion. When she told me that it was definitely cancer, all the blood rushed from my head and I felt like I was about to faint. That evening, Pete and I told our two older children about the diagnosis. My fourteen-year-old son asked if I was going to die. I told him that I didn't intend to. Little did I know, the diagnosis would get worse.

After the surgery, the pathology report showed that the cancer had spread to twelve lymph nodes. As I walked through the "valley of the shadow of death," Jesus became my Rock and my Fortress. The cares of this world and the love of things that had so easily entangled me fell by the wayside. God not only began to heal me physically, but also was doing a greater work in my heart.

Though I don't believe that God caused the cancer, I can truly say that I wouldn't change any of that heart-wrenching experience. The Lord revealed to me the sins of pride, materialism, and worldliness that I had let creep into my life. He showed me lovingly, yet truthfully, that I wasn't always the wonderful wife and mother I thought I was. More important, He opened my eyes to see what is truly important in life—my relationship with Him, my husband, and my family.

Such a devastating diagnosis can have a profound effect on a husband. Many decide that they can't take the pressure of such a serious and somewhat deforming disease and either leave or withdraw emotionally. Pete's response was amazing—he was changed. All through the ordeal, he was sensitive, loving, and caring toward me. The biggest change I saw in him was that his faith in the Lord grew ever deeper. His relationship with the Lord became not only intellectual, but also a heartfelt, emotional relationship with a healing Jesus.

Now we both realize that each day is a gift from God. We must never take each other and our love for granted. No longer is making Jesus the center of our marriage a cliché, but a privilege. As the psalmist declares, "I will say of the LORD, 'He is my refuge and my fortress, my God, in whom I trust.'"[36]

Patti holds a special place in my (Connie) heart—she's my cousin. During a blessed period of three years, we lived near one another, and our families attended the same church. Our kids played together, and our families enjoyed one another regularly. These memories remain some of my fondest. During that time, I couldn't help but notice how much Patti loved God. She was far more serious about Him than I was, and I wondered what made her that way. I just didn't quite "get it." She was—and still is—a tremendous inspiration to me.

When she faced cancer, I saw courage in her that could only come from God. I'll never forget something she shared with me about a year after her diagnosis. She said, "I wouldn't change a thing, even if I could. I have a closer relationship with God now than I ever have before. I know Him intimately. I'm thankful that this forced me to stop and regroup, and realize what's important in life."

Patti was living out 1 Thessalonians 5:18: "Give thanks in all circumstances, for this is God's will for you in Christ Jesus."

My mom often sees Patti, since they live fairly close to each other. Each time she sees her, she relates to me how "wonderful" she looks. "She just seems to be so peaceful about everything," my mom once said.

It's no wonder. She's living out God's will for her in Christ Jesus with a thankful heart—confident that the One who saw her through the valley of the shadow continues to hold her future in His hands.

Is Jesus an intimate Friend to you,
or merely a casual one?

Stargazing in the Darkest Nights

*Two Looked out from Prison Bars;
One Saw Mud, the Other, Stars.*

ANONYMOUS

*W*ouldn't it be lovely if everyone who touched our life was a stargazer…always looking on the bright side of things, forever seeing the best in people, refusing to let anything discourage or upset them? But life just isn't that way. God has made us all different. He knows what each person needs in her life to draw her closer to Himself. We look with dismay at the pruning shears He uses on every one of His children, when it is actually His intention to make us fruitful.[37] At one time or another all of us will seem to be a prisoner of circumstances. The outcome for you depends on your willingness to depend on God.

Several years ago, my husband was dealing with some difficult issues that caused him to become depressed, although I didn't recognize this at the time. Sad to say, I was focused on his surface behavior and didn't like what I saw. I had entered

189

into marriage as a lifelong commitment, but I was struggling to remember what I'd loved about him enough to marry him. I was shocked to realize that I had allowed my love to grow cold, and I knew I needed to do something about it. When I realized he was depressed, I began to understand that there was nothing I could do to make him "snap out of it." He was heartsick. And I was more so when I realized that *my* problem was lovelessness. This stunned me. I knew I needed to do something to salvage my love for my husband.

This was an eye-opening discovery, and I knew I couldn't do it on my own. I had tried and failed miserably. So I began praying in earnest for God to ignite my heart with a new love for my husband. That fall I signed up for a study on marriage in hopes that I would find something to grab on to. The Lord brought to my attention two areas:

The first was that when I serve my husband I actually serve Jesus![38] Knowing this took all the pressure off my husband to reciprocate or respond.[39] Serving my husband without expecting anything in return guarded me from becoming discouraged or disappointed. And as I began to serve my husband and family in this way, I found the ability to stop focusing on what he wasn't doing for me, and even the fact that he didn't seem to appreciate what I did for him.

The second thing God taught me was the importance of forgiveness. I didn't realize that when I refused to forgive, I was in effect imprisoning my husband.[40]

As I prayed for God's help, I experienced the beginnings of a new love for my husband. It was a deeper love than I had ever experienced before; it was agape love...love that is unconditional. Not only that, but my love for God grew tremendously. And I would need that in the years that followed.

During the next five years, we went through some devastating layoffs, with no work for months at a time. At those times, especially in the first year of unemployment, I learned a new lesson: *Be still and know that I am God.*[41] I tend to be confident of what I believe and think. As a woman and a mom, I want to be a "fixer." In times past, when I saw a problem I did my best to set it straight. That may be a good approach with a toddler, but it isn't what God intended for me as a wife. In our culture, there is an attitude that says women have all the answers, if only men would listen. Many times through those years, my mind was screaming solutions that appeared to be so clear to me. Unfortunately, God didn't inspire those thoughts. I could have been openly critical of my husband and his way of doing things. Thankfully, my prayer at that time was, *God, I want him to hear from You. If I am going to err, let me err on the side of not saying enough—don't let me say anything that isn't from You.*

God helped me hold my tongue and impressed me with the fact that He'd sent the Holy Spirit for my husband to give him direction. I'd been trying to take the Holy Spirit's place—how much sense does that make? When I did that, I might be saying things that sounded good, even sounded right. Like Job's self-righteous counselors, whose wisdom *sounded* right on target, I was relying on my own wisdom. Not only did my attempts not help, they actually drew my husband's focus off God and distracted him from God's whisperings. Time after time, I found myself biting my tongue. But I was praying a mile a minute for God to give him the answers he so desperately wanted.

I freely spoke expressions of love and support. I gave my husband constant assurances of my love and told him how much I needed him. I told him I'd never let him go. My husband needed to be touched—not only in a sexual sense, but physically touching his arm, neck, back, or face at every opportunity. These were the messages he needed to hear from me.

Now, looking back, I recognize that through this pruning process in my life, God was making it possible for me to learn how to rely solely on Him. Many times I cried out for Him to send someone else to come alongside us; I felt desperately alone. What I needed to learn, though, is that He is my sufficiency. Now I can see that that time deepened my love for both my husband and God. Our relationship continues to grow stronger every day. We are firmly committed to each other and believe that God works all things together for the good of those who love the Lord and are called according to His purpose.[42]

What our friend and her husband faced is one of the most unsettling of all tests—depression and job loss. These things rock our sense of security.

But the refining fire she went through has brought her forth as gold. If God allows joblessness, depression, or sorrow to enter your life, or if He shows you that you lack love for your husband, you don't have to be a prisoner of your circumstances. Because of Jesus, you can be a stargazer…for He declares of Himself, "I, Jesus, am…the bright Morning Star."[43] This kind of stargazing keeps your focus on Him and not yourself.

How are you responding to your husband's woundedness?

There Is No *IF* in *Love*

"I Tell You, Love...Help...Give Without Expecting a Return." —Luke 6:35, The Message

ANONYMOUS

*T*he saying goes that nothing in life is free. You go to the grocery store, fill your cart, and pay at the checkout stand. If you walk out without paying, you'll be stopped. Sadly, the same is often true in relationships. "I'll love you if you love me." But when we look at Jesus and the freedom He bought us by the shedding of His blood, we stand amazed. We are free to love the unlovely, free to love the unkind, free to be progressively made like Jesus when we do things His way. Because by His Spirit we have all the power we need to live a life of love...and have a heart like His!

My story is like countless women's stories: Somehow my love for my husband washed up on the shores of time. As I look back now, I see my Father's hand, my precious Father's hand....

Growing up, I never felt my parents' love and acceptance. No matter how hard I tried, I could never measure up to their expectations. When I married my husband, I thought the romance would last, but shortly after the "I dos," I began hearing the *d*-word—divorce. He wasn't happy. I did what almost everyone else does—I tried harder. I went to seminars, read books, sought advice, and went to studies geared toward becoming a woman more precious than jewels. Nothing worked. So I retreated. I spiraled down into a seven-year-long depression, followed by two years of anger and rage.

I felt that God had abandoned me and was punishing me for my failures. Toward the end of the depression, He showed me otherwise—that He wanted to expose the lies I'd believed since childhood and bring truth to the situation. He also showed me that I was not responsible for all the problems—as my husband had said—and I didn't need to carry the blame. This is where the anger and rage came into play.

How dare my husband blame me when he didn't attempt, and in fact refused, to meet my needs! He was 100 percent committed to *not* changing and told me, "This is the way I am. I'm not going to change. Deal with it."

My rage was directed not only toward him, but also toward God. God's commandment to love my enemies infuriated me. It had nothing to do with the other person—in this case, my husband. There were no loopholes.

But God began to show me Himself and His love for me. My anger grieved Him, yet His response to me was one of patience, love, and forgiveness. As this pattern continued, I became deeply touched and pleaded for Him to give me a heart like His for my husband. He granted my desire by taking me through six steps:

- **Confess** my part and be willing to change *me*.
- **Forgive my husband.** I cancelled the debt I felt he owed me. This freed me to move forward. When I forgave, I opened the door for God to work in his life.[44]

- Accept my reality.
- Relinquish all to Christ. I no longer had an agenda.
- Offer myself to Christ. All that I was, all that I hoped to be—my past pain and failures, my hopes and future—I offered to Him.
- Trust Him unquestioningly. He is worthy of my trust and will do what's best for me.

Since this turning point, I have endeavored to be Jesus to those around me, especially to my husband, who remains committed to not changing. I want God to continue to work in my heart and make me more like Jesus. I have surrendered my expectations. I endeavor to love and serve Him because that is what God has asked of me. It is a privilege to be a part of His kingdom work. I'm to follow Christ, not myself.

One day, I hope to hear my Father say, "Well done, good and faithful servant!"[45]

This woman has learned the marvelous lessons at the very heart of the gospel. It took her nine long years of depression, anger, and rage to discover the truths she shares with us: confession, forgiveness, acceptance, relinquishing all to Christ, offering herself to Him, and trusting Him for the results.

The writer of this story is my (Nancy) friend. She is the most peaceful woman I know, and now I understand why. "She will be kept in perfect peace, whose mind is stayed on Jesus, because she trusts."[46]

If you live with a presently unlovable spouse, may you learn how to live with him and love him with Jesus' love.

Wedding Day Small Talk?

"For Worse" and "in Sickness"

MARILYN AMSTUTZ

Do you remember what you were thinking as you stood just outside the sanctuary doors, waiting to walk down the aisle and become a wife? One woman wondered about her train—was it billowing gracefully behind her? Another friend shared that all she could think about was getting down the aisle so she could feel her groom's hand in hers. And another woman wasn't worried about herself at all. She was concentrating on her father, who had recently had a stroke. She wanted to do everything she could to make his walk down the aisle successful! Did the waiting groom have any idea what a gracious woman he was about to marry?

As the bride begins her walk down the aisle, the crowd rises to its feet. Everyone's eyes are upon her…in just a few moments she'll be reciting her vows. But will she be mindful of what she's promising?

It was that perfect time of year when all the trees and flowers are about to bloom. Our life paralleled the season. My husband was about to fulfill his lifelong dream. He had persevered through medical school, a grueling residency, and his payback time to the Air Force. We were looking forward to settling down with our preschool-age girls. I was consumed with the details of building our new home, and Kent was daydreaming about the private practice he was going to join.

But just as spring storms arrive suddenly, with horrific force, and sometimes leave behind great devastation, our family was hit with news that left us reeling. It changed our plans and profoundly challenged our faith.

During Kent's discharge physical, some abnormal results were found. A few weeks later we had the shocking news— Kent had chronic liver disease and the only cure was a transplant. Immediately, the Air Force whisked us off to Texas to see specialists and to discuss Kent's career. The doctors anticipated a liver transplant within a year. We were assured of medical coverage, but only if Kent remained on active duty.

Our reactions were quite different. Kent felt a loss of control that made him depressed and angry. Not only had he lost his health, but he had also lost his career dream. I experienced initial feelings of grief and loss, but God reminded me of His Word: "I know the plans I have for you...plans to prosper you and not to harm you, plans to give you hope and a future."[47] This promise became my unwavering foundation for the next six years. I firmly believed that God would get us through whatever awaited us. Holding on to that belief was probably the best thing that I did for my husband.

To a certain degree, Kent depended on me to support him emotionally and spiritually. At that low point in his life, he expected only sickness and death ahead of him. I couldn't support him without God's help, and I knew from past experiences that He would always be near.

Within weeks, God gave me an occasion to trust Him again by answering a prayer for a home. Kent had limited amounts of energy, so I set about house hunting. This was the beginning of many situations that necessitated independence on my part. I prayed, *Lord, I feel like Abraham's servant looking for a wife for Isaac. I know You have a house for us. Please guide me.* And He did. The first house I saw was for sale by owner. It was attractive and welcoming. The man who met me at the door explained that they had to move as soon as possible. Just before my arrival, he had fervently prayed that God would send a buyer. How like the Lord to encourage both of us! That evening the house was ours. For the next four years, we lived in a place that served as a reminder of God's faithfulness.

Kent experienced all the stages of grieving. I was not aware of the extent to which disease affects emotions. My initial attempts to encourage him usually ended in either tears or angry disagreements. God was working on our weak areas. I had to learn to be sympathetic without allowing his sorrow to immobilize me. Kent later acknowledged that my positive outlook had spurred him to get up and go to work every day. Eventually he accepted his illness as part of God's plan.

Our relationship grew deeper. We reaffirmed our love for each other and shared things that may have been left unsaid under normal circumstances. Kent began to see God's plans for his future. The Air Force allowed him to pursue a fellowship in developmental pediatrics in Washington. Kent's new upbeat outlook was contagious, and we were all pleased with the move.

For four years, Kent experienced relatively good health, but I became concerned when, on a family vacation, he uncharacteristically relinquished most of the driving to me. He slept most of our days away. He didn't feel well. He had little patience with the girls or me and would have unreasonable outbursts of anger. This was not the husband and father we normally saw. I taught the girls to recognize the difference between Daddy talking and the disease talking.

Upon returning home, the impact of Kent's disease hit full force. He began vomiting blood. Suddenly, my husband was in ICU. He was in and out of the hospital three times in one month. The doctors worried that he could not withstand more episodes like that. Kent was put on the liver transplant list. We were now in crisis mode.

At this point, Kent was physically wasted, cognitively impaired, and anxious that a liver would not become available. The challenge of helping a sick husband while trying to parent the girls and run the household was relieved by the dear friends God gave us. They watched, fed, and entertained the girls. Neighbors did the yard work. Our Sunday school class brought food. Whenever I became exhausted, my parents would arrive from Canada and take over. We were so grateful.

In spite of our disrupted life, we attempted to raise the girls normally. We spent holidays in the hospital, celebrating in Daddy's room. We claimed the hospital's outdoor dining area as ours for the summer. We learned to enjoy simple family pleasures. Life went on for the four of us, even if it wasn't how we'd planned.

As Kent's health worsened, it was upsetting to see him in that condition. I reminded the family that God had promised to see us through. I searched the Bible for verses of hope and shared them. The girls learned the verse that tells us that God's strength is sufficient. If I found them crying, I would remind them of that. If they saw me crying, they would remind me. Nightly we would think of one thing God had done to cheer us up that day. Then we would thank Him and ask for strength to continue. And for a new liver for Kent!

The very day that I thought I could not go on for one more minute was the day we received the long-awaited call. They had a liver for Kent! I will never forget it. After a successful surgery, Kent looked at me with a sly smile and said, "Honey, I'm back! And I'm as sharp as a tack!"

True to His Word, God saw Marilyn and Kent through the worst of times. They had their plans, but God showed them His. They saw firsthand that His plans were for good and not evil. They are living testimonies to God's sufficiency and strength.

Kent and Marilyn meant what they said on their wedding day. When they said "for better or worse" and "in sickness and in health," they literally meant till death do us part.

Does your husband know, without a doubt, that you'll be there for him for better, for worse, till death do you part?

Freedom!

If Your Forgiveness Is Based on Whether He "Deserves" It,
You're Living in a Prison of Your Own Making

ANONYMOUS

*D*id your mother ever make you and a sibling "kiss and make up"? Mine (Connie) did. Whenever my sisters and I argued, Mom would actually make us kiss one another's cheek and make up. Usually this occurred between my sister Bev and me. We were just eighteen months apart and spent a huge amount of time together. Most of our times together were fun—but not all of them!

"It's against the law to torture your kids," we'd say, but Mom never seemed too worried about the law coming to our house and hauling her away. "Okay, fine. Let's just get it over with." So Bev and I would stand as far apart as we could possibly get from each other and still be able to peck the other's cheek. The fact that my family has no estrangements today is due in large part, I think, to a mother who trained us at an early age to set things right, even though we didn't appreciate it then.

I (Nancy) wasn't a child when I learned about genuine forgiveness. I'd been married for over twenty years and thought forgiveness depended on how I felt. But I was so wrong. When I first heard that a woman wasn't to let the sun go down on her *anger, I honestly thought,* What fun is that? *I'd literally stand at the window and check the sun's progress, and then, right before it went down, I'd force myself to forgive Ray for whatever I'd been holding against him that day. I may not have been a child, but I was certainly acting like one!*

Forgiveness is an issue that Jesus addresses over and over again in Scripture. It was, and is, a big deal to Him. To disregard this issue is one of the most foolish things you could ever do. His Word tells us that we're to forgive quickly, completely, and often. This can sometimes be a challenge—especially in marriage.

I met my husband the first day of college. He was intelligent, interesting, funny, and considerate. *Who is this man? I have never met anyone like him!* I thought. We fell in love and were married fours year later.

We had a beautiful, simple wedding and drove to a nearby resort for what seemed a magical honeymoon. I felt like a princess, but the magic was soon cut short. On the way home, our car died alongside the highway, and right then and there my husband threw a first-class fit. As he yelled, stomped, and turned red with anger, I stood with my mouth hanging open. Again I was thinking, *Who is this man? I have never met anyone like him!*

I tried to convince him that we could wait for help or walk down the road to a house, but there was no reasoning with him. I told him things would be fine and suggested he was overreacting. He just became angrier and yelled at *me!* I was shocked. He had hurt my feelings and now I was angry, too. Things deteriorated rapidly, but he eventually cooled down and we were on our way. I decided that this outburst was caused by the stress of getting married. Like any young and naive bride, I decided it probably wouldn't happen again.

As the years went by, he was thoughtful and loving in many ways. We had lots of good times. But there were too many times when he became unnecessarily frustrated and angry. It didn't matter if the problems were big or small. I finally realized that this was just his way of letting off steam. He wasn't intentionally cruel—rather, he just got mad and yelled at whoever was nearby, which was usually me.

Having children was great, but of course along with children comes many crises. He often turned them into angry events. I frequently felt I was living with a madman and longed for a peaceful home. Sometimes I fantasized about running away to a quiet place—anyplace—but I had children to care for and didn't want a divorce.

During this time, I became an emotional accounting expert. I faithfully kept a record of every hurtful moment. I kept long lists in my mind of all the times I was right and he was wrong. I dwelled on his faults. I was busy keeping impeccable records. And I was miserable.

He began to realize that his outbursts were causing some problems at work. He had just been promoted and his new boss mentored him in many areas—one being anger control. He began to change. Growing older had caused him to mellow some, too. But even though he was improving, I was still holding on to my past hurts.

At this time I was growing in my knowledge of and love for the Lord. I knew that I should forgive my husband, and I tried. But he had caused so much turmoil and mental anguish in our family that I thought he didn't deserve to be totally forgiven. He was sorry, but was he sorry enough? Did he really realize how much he had hurt us? I felt it was my job to keep reminding him. Plus, if I were to really forgive and forget, would he take this as an invitation to return to his old ways?

Then I heard some startling words on forgiveness that pierced my heart:

- *"Forgive others as God forgives you."*[48] Of course, this verse was not new to me, but I think it was the first time I felt God speaking directly to me about this. I could forgive friends and other family members, but him? I was reminded of all the times I had failed Jesus and He kept forgiving me—and even forgetting! Could I do that?
- *Failing to forgive fully is not forgiving at all.* I was often willing to forgive my husband's small sins, but not his big ones.
- *Don't wait to forgive until you feel they deserve it...forgive them now.* God commands us to forgive one another, period![49] He does not add "if they deserve it" or "when they are sorry enough." This is how I'd been living.
- *Forgiveness is a choice, not a feeling.* It is not a sign of weakness to freely forgive. It is a sign of God's strength working through me. I once heard it said that the will is the engine of the train and the emotions are the caboose. Guess which one powers the train? Too often we give our cabooses way too much power. The other person doesn't even have to be sorry, but I can still choose to forgive.
- *Forgiveness doesn't mean I wasn't hurt.* But it does mean I'll choose to forgive regardless of my feelings.

With much prayer and with Christ's power within me, I have forgiven my husband and put the past behind us. When he has "one of those days," he still vents on occasion, and I remind myself of how far he has come and thank God for his progress—and for my own, too!

Learning to forgive is the best thing I have ever done for my marriage. I no longer live with a constant knot in my stomach. I am free to love and enjoy my husband in the way God intended me to.

Our skies aren't always blue. Of course there are still a few rainy days now and then. But the really angry storms seem far behind us, and I give the glory and praise to God.

We have known this woman for years and admire her warm, gentle spirit. A few days after she wrote her story, she followed it up with this note:

> *Last week, after I had written this, I was becoming irritated with my husband after quite a few little outbursts. I was thinking that I had forgiven him just about enough for one weekend. Oh, how quickly we can slip back into our old ways! Then, on Monday, I became jealous about a work-related party he was going to. I said some ugly things. God immediately spoke to me. He reminded me that He forgives me of all my sins—how could I do less for my beloved husband? Is God good or what? He keeps me moving forward. I am His creation—a continual work in progress.*

Yes, a continual work in progress—that's what each of us is. God's Word tells us that as we become more and more like Jesus, we're being transformed from one degree of glory to another.[50] Isn't that a wonderful thought!

Is there something you're holding against your husband that needs to be forgiven? Maybe it's something he said or did, or maybe it's simply the way he is. Ask God to help you be a true forgiver, and be transformed to another degree of glory.

Are you holding anything against your husband that needs to be forgiven?

When Things Go Terribly Wrong

*Big Dreams, Bright Hopes, and Whirlwind Courtships
Don't Always Lead to Blissful Marriages*

TRISH FINLEY

*What's a woman to do when her husband is injured,
released from his job, becomes deeply depressed and suicidal, has
chronic pain, checks into a mental hospital, and leaves her alone to
parent the children and make a living for the family? These days, it
takes a whole lot less to drive a woman to file for a divorce. How in
the world can one person handle events so desperate? There is only
one answer—through the power of the Author of love Himself,
Jesus Christ. Only He can help you love this way. Is it possible to
live happily ever after when things go terribly wrong? Trish knows
the answer firsthand.*

John and I were attracted to each other from the moment we
met, and we were married within two months. The day of our
wedding, I had a few moments alone in the church. I knelt

and asked God to give me wisdom and stamina to keep the vows I was about to make.

Little did I realize our lives would hit such rocky spots. After two years, our first baby was stillborn. We never got to see or hold him. As the days passed, John went into such a depressed state that he wouldn't talk to me. He was working as a groundskeeper at the same cemetery where our son was buried, which was very unsettling for him.

Within days of our baby's death, John seriously injured his back. After his hospital stay, he was moved home, still in traction. A week later, he was rushed to the hospital with a bleeding ulcer.

During the next eight years, we had two children and I began teaching school. But again John became seriously ill—developing viral meningitis. He was hospitalized for seven weeks and received heavy medication to help with the pain.

I didn't understand why God was letting this situation happen. The Lord reminded me of my promise—"in sickness and in health, till death do us part." Because John wasn't improving, we decided to take him to the Mayo Clinic. The doctors found that an opening into his small intestine was closed, so another surgery was performed. After two weeks, I had to return to teaching. John became bitter and upset that I had abandoned him, although family members were faithful in caring for him. When John returned home, he was still in so much pain that it began to affect his mental status. He began to talk about suicide and was admitted to a mental health facility for the first of several stays. I cried out to God and wondered if I could remain in my marriage.

For the next ten years John continued to rely on medication to help with the depression and his constant pain. God gave me enormous grace to love my husband through all of this.

I sought counseling at our church and learned that everything goes through God's hands before it comes to us. I also learned that if I wanted to increase my significance, I had to focus my energies on significant activities...those that would remain for eternity.

Once again John had become too dependent on drugs for pain and had to enter a mental hospital. This time he came to grips with some of his fears and slowly started coming back to reality. The love and gentleness that had been buried deep inside for years began to pour out of him once again. My relationship with John has become precious. And for the first time in years, John's jovial personality is returning.

A friend gave me the devotional *31 Days of Praise* by Ruth Myers.[51] My favorite selection is day 23, which reminds me to thank God for His plan to use for good the struggles that the people I love face, including their disappointing choices and their unwise or even harmful ways of thinking and living. I love the Lord and praise Him for His continual prompting to endure, love, and care for John. A favorite promise from His Word is, "Be not afraid or dismayed at this great multitude; for the battle is not yours, but God's."[52]

Isn't this an incredible love story?[53] God has taught Trish to persevere. She has a sweet sensitivity to the afflicted because of the "school of suffering" she has attended for the last twenty-seven years. Just recently God used Trish as a catalyst for a young woman to receive Christ. She has since befriended the girl, bought her a Bible, and helped her find a church.

Trials can either break us or make us conduits for the love of

God. Trish's path may seem hard to walk, but she is marching on, running and not growing weary, knowing that one day she will fall into the arms of God Himself.

How do you handle the cares and afflictions of your husband?

This Will Be Your Husband's Favorite Chapter!

Sex Between a Husband and Wife Is One of God's Holiest Gifts

ANONYMOUS

or the past several years, we've taught a study on marriage. One of the things we openly address is sex. In fact, we've had numerous women tell us that they've never heard such frank discussion in all their lives! Each week, their homework is to go home and put into practice what they learned in class. You can imagine the feigned moaning and groaning, as well as laughter, that arises when class is over and the women are headed home, homework in hand.

The following week, though, many of the women come back just glowing. "I had no idea just how big a deal sex is to my husband," woman after woman would tell us. "He was thrilled to death with this week's 'homework.' He says this class is a husband's dream come true!"

Yes, sex is a big deal to a man. And it should be to you as well!

*You may be surprised to hear, as many in our class are, that sex
was actually God's idea in the first place. In fact, it was the first
thing He spoke about to Adam and Eve.*

One of the best things I ever did for my marriage was to make
our intimate relationship a high priority. For the first ten years
of our marriage, we struggled in this area. It wasn't that we
had any major physical or emotional problems, but more that
we were self-conscious, self-centered, and perhaps a bit naive,
especially me.

For a long time, I didn't know that sex was God's idea
and that it is a gift to us in marriage. I was surprised to see
how much God said about it in His Word, and I was flabber-
gasted to discover that a woman could be sensual and godly
at the same time. I'd always thought these two words couldn't
be used in the same sentence! But God rejoices greatly in this
intimate physical union between husband and wife, which is
part of His plan for making us one.

In my immaturity, I never realized how important the
sexual relationship is to a man. I learned that sex is a huge
need for a husband—emotionally and physically.

After I started meeting my husband's needs in this regard,
every other area of our marriage improved over time. The
walls started coming down and the lines of communication
opened. My husband became more tender toward me and
was more responsive to my needs as well.

Things didn't change overnight. I spent many hours talking to God about it. I learned that "the wife's body does not
belong to her alone, but also to her husband,"[54] and that the
same is true for the husband:

It's good for a man to have a wife, and for a woman to have a husband. Sexual drives are strong, but marriage is strong enough to contain them and provide for a balanced and fulfilling sexual life in a world of sexual disorder. The marriage bed must be a place of mutuality—the husband seeking to satisfy his wife, the wife seeking to satisfy her husband. Marriage is not a place to "stand up for your rights." Marriage is a decision to serve the other, whether in bed or out. Abstaining from sex is permissible for a period of time if you both agree to it, and if it's for the purposes of prayer and fasting—but only for such times. Then come back together again. Satan has an ingenious way of tempting us when we least expect it. I'm not, understand, commanding these periods of abstinence—only providing my best counsel if you should choose them.[55]

Another verse that changed my thinking completely was: "The man and his wife were both naked, and they felt no shame."[56] I had to rid my mind of old mindsets and misconceptions and align my thoughts with God's perspective.

As I have given my body as a "gift" to my husband, we have both enjoyed a very fulfilling intimate relationship that keeps getting better all the time. I also feel a deeper love for my husband than I did when we were newlyweds!

Best of all, I feel that God is at the center of our marriage. I thank Him for giving us this precious gift of intimacy.

After your relationship with God, your marriage is your first and most important ministry. And the sexual aspect of this union is something you should hold tenderly and cherish dearly. Here are some practical things you may want to introduce into your marriage:

- Become the initiator! This is especially important if you have been neglecting your husband's sexual needs.
- Tell your husband what you enjoy, and ask what brings him pleasure.
- Ask your husband to rate from 1 to 10 your present nightly wardrobe. Sweat pants and socks are for the gym!
- Ask God to help you restore this area of marriage.
- Tell your husband what a wonderful lover he is. This will build him up like little else.

How long has it been since you told your husband what a wonderful lover he is?

My Cup
Runneth Over

*A marriage is much like a garden. It needs to be
tended, weeded, watered, and cared for. So often
a woman cares for all the gardens in her life far
better than the garden of her marriage. Before
long, it's a mess! But often when she purposes to
get her marriage garden in order, opportunities
arise that she never dreamed possible.*

If You Want to
Be Used by God

...First Learn to Serve

ROSEMARY JENSEN
GENERAL DIRECTOR, RAFIKI FOUNDATION, INC.

It is so amazing how God trains wives for leadership. It's only when she understands and undertakes the primary role God has given her that she is placed in the position of leadership that brings eternal glory to Him. And as Rosemary Jensen learned first-hand, the wife's role is to be a helper to her husband. Look it up! "And the LORD God said, 'It is not good for the man to be alone. I will make a helper suitable for him.'"[57] When I (Connie) heard this, I went home and looked up that verse in every version I could find...and sure enough, it's in all of them! The Bible also says, "Wives, be subject to your husbands [subordinate and adapt yourselves to them], as is right and fitting and your proper duty in the Lord."[58] Be inspired as you read Rosemary's story.

In 1954, I married the most wonderful man in the world. At least, that's what I believed with all my heart at the time. Later

I found out that he had a few minor flaws, but I was shocked to find out that I had even bigger flaws. We're still flawed, but God put us in circumstances to refine us. He placed my husband and me in Tanzania, East Africa, for nine years. Those years made big changes in my life.

You see, at about the age of seventeen, I had been given the desire to be a missionary. In His grace, God gave me Bob, who wanted to be a medical missionary. What could be better than that? I would be given the opportunity to tell others about God while with my husband.

What the Lord wanted to teach me was that He was not so interested in my telling others about Him as He was in Bob's work for Him. It was God's plan for Bob to build a 450-bed hospital on the slopes of Mount Kilimanjaro. The Kilimanjaro Christian Medical Centre is there today as an example of what God can do. But Bob couldn't have done this most important work without my full support.

I had to be the wife who was willing to be left alone for weeks at a time, the mother of his three children, his secretary, his hostess to constant houseguests, and most of all his encourager when things got rough.

Although I was able to do *some* teaching, there was little time for me to teach others about God. I was thrilled with what my husband was doing, but I struggled because the tasks I had been assigned by God weren't my first choice. Had God put desires within me only to thwart them?

What I didn't realize until years later was that God was teaching me through those years of aloneness the need to depend on Him for everything. It was my not-so-willing submission to God that taught me to know Christ in His submissive role to His Father's will. To my amazement, I found that supporting my husband in the work God had called him to do brought Bob and me closer together. We were building something for the needy people of Tanzania, which strengthened the bond between us. Once I had learned the lesson that in order to lead one must first learn to serve, God was ready to fulfill my heart's desire to teach others about Him—with the full support of my husband.

On our return to the United States, I was introduced to Bible Study Fellowship and given the joy of teaching the Word of God. My only regret was that my teaching was not in Africa. Eventually, I became the executive director of BSF and served in that capacity for twenty years. During those years, my husband and I and a few others started the Rafiki Foundation, and I became its general director. Upon retirement from BSF in June 2000, I was free to serve in Rafiki full-time and to encourage Bob in some writing he had always wanted to do. And Bob is right there supporting me in everything God is calling me to do.

Each year we have together gets sweeter because we are *mutually supportive* in the work that God ordained for us.

The impact that Rosemary Jensen has had on my (Nancy) life continues to this day.

In 1987, the Lord providentially led Anne Graham Lotz, who was the teaching leader of Bible Study Fellowship in Raleigh, North Carolina, to choose me as her replacement. I went to BSF headquarters in San Antonio, Texas, for a week of training. I recall assuring Rosemary that I would do everything by the manual. She looked at me for a moment and said, "Well, be creative, dear!"

When we began sending letters out asking women to write a chapter for this book, I immediately thought of Rosemary. I began my letter: "Rosemary, you probably don't remember me, but..." (Fifteen years had elapsed.) Not long after, I was humbled to read her note. "Well, of course I remember you…and continue to be creative!" What a marvelous leader she is and how grateful I am for her influence in my life and around the world.

Can you see how God can mightily use a woman who is a godly wife? It is precious to note that as Rosemary sowed support into her relationship with Bob, she is now reaping support from him.

Are you a godly wife?
Do you support God's plans for your husband?

"Your Wife Needs a Pastoral Call!"

Pastors' Wives Are Often the Unsung Heroes of the Faith

RUTH DENHART

What a joy it is to become friends with a woman of faith. I (Nancy) had a brand-new Bible and a newfound desire to know the truth about God. My hunger only deepened as I began a study Ruth taught. I marveled as she spoke with such wisdom—she seemed to know God! No wonder she spoke with such authority. She did know God, and because of her deep commitment to Him, she was a Proverbs 31 kind of wife. Ruth and Charles's marriage and their interactions with each other were joys to behold. In a day when marriage is often taken lightly, it's wonderful to hear from a woman who has stayed the course and is willing to share what she has learned.

It was only thirty-seven cents, but my husband said it was the best money he ever spent. Thus began a marriage that is still intact and in fact quite vital. My pastor had agreed, after a facetious discussion we were having just before I left for college, that when I got married, his honorarium would be just thirty-seven cents. So when Charles and I married, the pastor accepted just thirty-seven cents because he said "a deal is a deal."

Charles and I established a solid foundation for marriage with the conviction that this covenant was indeed "till death do us part." We didn't have a Plan B if things didn't work out. We understood that it wasn't our job to try to change the other person.

Over the years, we have enjoyed reading aloud to one another, usually at bedtime. One of the most enjoyable is a book of short stories by William E. Barton called *Safed the Sage*. In one parable, the wife, Keturah, suggests to her husband that it would be better and more orderly if he would place his shoes in the closet rather than under the bed. His response is:

> Thou wast not made as I was out of dust of the earth.
> Thirty and three years ago did God cause a deep sleep
> to fall upon me. Then took He one of my ribs and
> made Thee. And Thou camest into my life and next to
> mine heart, not as something from the world without,
> but as that which already belonged to me, and must
> be mine as long as the heavens endure. Nevertheless,
> of all my rips art Thou the most unquiet.[59]

The conversation continues with each extolling the other's virtues and Safed making certain condescension and asking for "a little latitude in the matter of the shoes." Keturah responds with, "I verily believe that there are worse husbands even than Thou." And they both go about their business, happy.

Sometimes we can read the signs; other times we might need to be more subtle. When our daughter and her husband were expecting their first tiny treasure, they had a wall hanging with moveable figures of a man, woman, child, dog, and a coop. One only had to glance at it to see who, if anyone, was in the doghouse. Sometimes it was the baby! Using a soft approach is the better part of wisdom. Areas that might cause dissension can be amicably discussed, and this is best done with a sense of humor. We ask the Lord for a measure of common sense and a sense of humor, and if we lack wisdom we ask God and He provides it.[60]

When we were a young family in a new place of ministry, my husband, being a very goal-oriented person, was gone day and night getting acquainted with the people, the church, and the town. It seemed he would wear himself down, and it was lonely for the children and me. I wanted to tell him that if he did himself in, the church could get another pastor, but his family would be in big trouble! Instead, I put a sign on the refrigerator that said, "Your wife needs a pastoral call." The Lord, no doubt, inspired that action—He used it to change Charles's approach to pastoral ministry, and it encouraged him to always block out time for us.

It seemed reasonable that if we chose to spend the rest of our lives together, we should become best friends and enjoy all the perks that exist in such a relationship. Over the years, we discovered that best friends love and support each other and build each other up. The best resource we have is prayer—if change is needed, God can change situations and He can change us.[61] We have experienced God's "awesome deeds"[62] of healing and even sparing of life in answer to prayer. He is a miracle-working God!

I marvel at the way God has directed our lives. I love how

He once planted the thought in each of us, separately, that He would be leading us from one pastorate to a new place. The whole process was so orchestrated by the Lord that we both had complete peace and confirmation in the decision. In our early years, the Lord impressed upon me that in the pulpit, this man was my pastor and it was always so. Besides being my pastor, he has been my inspiration to read, study, and love the Word of God.

It was important to our family for home to be a sanctuary. We did plenty of entertaining and the children's friends came and went, but there was this place, *home*, where the family was free to be comfortable. I love the Psalm that says, "I will walk in my house with blameless heart."[63] That is my continuing desire. My great yardstick for all relationships is given by One who knows: "Do to others what you would have them do to you."[64] And, by His grace, that is my plan. My journey with Charles has brought me more joy than I can possibly say.

When the topic "the best thing I ever did for my marriage" came up, Ruth's first inclination was to say, "I stayed." But instead she shares lessons the Lord has given her along the way.

My (Nancy) first encounter with a godly woman was with Ruth. She is gentle, loving, and very funny. I can say with all my heart that the best thing Charles ever did for his marriage was to marry such a Christlike woman, and the same is true for Ruth. It was their example that prodded me to know Jesus personally.

Does your example prod others to want to know more of Jesus?

The Greatest of These

*Can Your Husband Say That He
Feels Deeply Loved by You?*

DEBI CONDRA

*W*hen I was a young girl, my (Connie) parents would often tell me that they loved me. Sometimes I'd ask why. "Because we just do," they'd say. "Nothing you can do or say will ever change that." I've often felt that one reason I had so little trouble accepting the fact that God loved me was because my parents loved me so greatly. My daughter has a college friend whose parents didn't treat her this way. Not surprisingly, she wonders if there really is a God, and if there is, why would He love her?

Love is a powerful thing, especially in the life of the man you married.

I was elated when I was asked to write something for my best friend's book. Then it dawned on me that I actually had to think of something to write! I wondered if in my twenty-five years of marriage I had ever done anything really great for my husband. So I asked him. And the best thing? You might be surprised…

Twenty years ago, my husband and I left for Papua, New Guinea, with a toddler and, unbeknownst to us, another on the way. Our goal was to translate the New Testament for a people group that didn't have it in their mother tongue. Three months after the birth of our daughter, we flew to a small island called New Ireland Island, where we built a house out of jungle materials with the help of our new friends, the Patpatar people. We bathed and washed our clothes in a stream that ran by the side of our house. We caught rainwater in a tank for drinking. I made our food from scratch and provided the medical care for our family, as well as the rest of the village, with help from a doctor via radio. We didn't have electricity except what was provided by a solar panel, which charged a car battery. No TV, no movies, no fast food, no recreation except what we made for ourselves. When our children became older, school was held in a bamboo building with Mom as the teacher.

For sixteen years, this is how we lived. We had sickness and even brushes with death. We knew sorrow, loneliness, and feelings of inadequacy, as well as the joy of a close-knit family and an incredible sense of purpose. Through it all, we were blessed immeasurably.

We learned the Patpatar language, reduced it to writing, and finally published the Patpatar New Testament, *No Sigar Kunubus*.

It might sound like things went pretty smoothly for us over those years—unless you were there! I was less than supermom and way less than superwife. Though I did my best, I sometimes wanted to quit. However, the way I lived somehow spoke love to my husband. He said that no matter what, I stood by him, was faithful to him, and most of all loved him. He said that even when things got really bad, he could depend on my love.

I once heard of a famous missionary who was asked, "How did you do what you did?" He said, "I was a 'plodder.' I did the next thing that needed doing."

Too often, people think of love as the grand things: roses, gifts, a surprise trip, an elegant dinner. But even more, love is about the "plodding" things: wiping a nose, fixing a meal, making pizza from next to nothing, and yes, washing clothes in the river without complaining. It means living above my circumstances and being content with the wonderful mate God has gifted me with.

I'm still not supermom or superwife. But I endeavor every day to let my husband know I love him. Certainly there are the grand times, but there are far more days when I find that I must simply place one foot in front of the other.

I now know that it is in the plodding that God has used me most, for that is how my husband was able to see that "the greatest of these is love."[65]

Debi and Ed have been like family to us (Connie) for sixteen years. Debi is a woman of prayer—in fact, our friendship is the result of her prayers. For over a year she asked the Lord to give her a friend when they went on furlough. She'd gone months at a time without having an English-speaking friend and had grown lonely for some-one to share her heart with. My family and I are the blessed recipients of her answered prayer, for God not only hooked our hearts together as sisters, but our husbands and children bonded in a special way. God did what Ephesians 3:20 says He can do—far more than we can even ask or imagine.

When the Patpatar New Testament was finally finished and was being dedicated, Ed stood up to say a few words. He thanked many and finally turned toward Debi. As he looked at the woman who had stood by his side for seventeen long years, he was too overcome with emotion to utter a single word. He cried. She cried. Everyone cried. Surely the Lord was pleased at the way Debi had come alongside Ed, partnering with him through it all. She had grabbed hold of Ed's dream, and somewhere in the mix, it became her dream as well. She once said to me, "If something happened to Ed, with God's help I could finish our work."

Love is many things. And of the many things love is, undoubtedly one of those is a woman who gets out of bed every morning and purposes to let her husband know she considers it a privilege to be his wife.

Does your husband feel deeply loved by you, day after day?

The Home Builder

Choosing the Right Builder Makes All the Difference

LOTTIE KROGH

t's so intriguing to us that the person in this book who has been married the longest—fifty-seven years—has given us the shortest story of all. Anyone who has ever met Lottie is inspired by her wisdom, challenged by her faith, and struck by the deep love she has for Jesus. Lottie's husband died three years ago, and even though his loss has grieved her, she continues serving the Lord with passion. She is a walking testimony of His grace. What a blessing to know a woman like this!

The turning point in my marriage came many years before marriage was even part of my thinking.

By age fourteen, my life had fallen apart. My two-year-old sister had died, and shortly afterward, Dad decided that Mom and us kids would no longer be part of his life. After the divorce, my dad attempted to kidnap me. This caused endless fears and emotional trauma for me, and I worried constantly about the future.

Sometime later, I attended a service given by a group of young people. They spoke of experiencing God's love and personal care after committing their lives to Jesus. It was then that God made it clear that *He* was the one I needed in my life.[66] From that night forward I have known peace, as well as the assurance of God's love. The fear was gone.

I met Oakley in the church choir. On May 6, 1944, we were married and ten months later, his B-17 crew flew to Italy to take part in World War II. We were separated for fifteen months, but we were faithful and true to each other.[67]

When the war was over, we began our family. God gave us three boys and two girls. I had come to learn that the woman has a unique role in building the home through the wisdom God gives, no matter where that home is built or how many live under its roof. A grandmother lived with us for eighteen years.

We lived in a small home with just one bathroom and no TV. We struggled financially and later had physical problems, but we prayed through it all. After fifty-seven years of marriage, I look back and realize the turning point in my marriage was at age fourteen.[68] It was then that I began to be the person God wanted me to be.

Success in marriage is more than finding the right person; it is becoming the right person. Lottie allowed the Lord to build her house: "Unless the LORD builds the house, its builders labor in vain."[69] He was not only her Savior and Lord, but also the most welcomed Family Member. Lottie's generation has been called the Greatest Generation. They went through the Great Depression and four wars. She is a woman who can look back on the broad strokes of her life, knowing that she has brought Him honor and glory. She would never say this of herself because she is such a humble woman, but we know it to be true.

Are you becoming the right person in your marriage?

A Texas Girl and an Oklahoma Boy

Some Childhood Decisions Can Impact Lives for Eternity

ANN COODY

*H*ave you even been around a woman who is truly gracious, whose very presence instills in you the desire for that same grace in your own life? I (Connie) have had such a woman in my life for as long as I can remember, my aunt Ann. If you asked anyone who knows her well to describe her, the number one adjective you'd hear is gracious. Ann is graciousness personified.

I first saw the secret to her graciousness almost twenty years ago. She was spending some time with us in San Antonio to be near her mother, who lay dying in a nearby hospital. The first time I went up to sit with Ann between visiting hours in the ICU, I found her seated in the waiting room, reading from a small Bible. This struck me as rather odd. Why would she read her Bible when there was other, more interesting material to choose from—like magazines?

Obviously, Ann knew far more about interesting reading material than I did! And she knew God in a way I didn't. She knew Him intimately. This is what made her so gracious. When a woman has *an intimate relationship with her Savior, her life has His hand-prints all over it, especially her marriage…*

The best thing I ever did for my marriage happened when I was just ten years old!

I trusted Jesus Christ as my Savior and gave my life to Him. I knew at that young age that I wanted Christ to direct my life, and as I grew older I asked Him to direct me to the person He wanted me to marry…and He did! How else could a girl from Texas meet a boy from Oklahoma on a blind date, then later move halfway around the world—only to come back and find him there?

Through forty-three years of marriage, two wonderful children, a precious grandchild, many joys, and some problems and heartaches, Dale and I have always known that God led us together and have counted our commitment to one another a commitment first to Him. Yes, there have been problems, but our almighty Counselor saw us through each and every one.

Each day I pray for our marriage, read God's Word, and ask Him to handle things that might be difficult to talk to my husband about. Do I slip and fall? All the time. But Jesus is always there to catch me.

It is such joy to be married to a Christian. Dale and I are opposites in many ways, but our love for God and desire for His will for our lives is stronger than all of our differences. If you are married to a Christian man, don't take it for granted! This is something many women long for. Dale and I are so thankful for how God has grown us together and changed us both—merging our lives into one.

I've found that in my marriage it helps me tremendously to:

- give it all to Christ—and this includes my husband!
- trust God to know what's best—He's much better at this than I am.
- seek His forgiveness when mistakes are made and be quick to forgive others.
- ask God to love Dale through me. Something precious occurs when a woman is willing to be the vessel of God's love to her husband.

So the best thing I did for my marriage I did at ten years of age, but I've continued doing every day since—I ask God to direct my life and make me pleasing to Him.

Ann is not only gracious, but is also a woman of remarkable beauty. Her greatest beauty is within—for she has cultivated an inner beauty in which the Lord delights. For the past several years she's been active in the educational field and is currently involved in the political field as well. Yet she'd be the first to tell you that the most important thing she can ever do with her life is to please God in all she does.

What would you say is the most important thing in your life?

God's Amazing Grace

If I find in myself a desire which no experience in this world can satisfy, the most probable explanation is that I was made for another world. —C. S. Lewis

BRENDA WHEALY

*E*ver been tired? Of course! We all have. Sometimes we can be so weary at night that we're almost too tired to actually get up off the couch and go to bed.

There's something about spiritual tiredness, though, that is especially exhausting. Nothing more quickly tires us spiritually than trying to do things in our own strength. It wears a person out, yet many spend months—even years—in that mode. Sometimes entire lifetimes can be spent just "trying harder."

A few months ago we heard the story of a kind elderly man, who at his deathbed tearfully said to his pastor, "I hope I go to heaven—I've spent all my life trying as hard as I know how to get there."

As the pastor shared this story, his voice broke and he had to stop and compose himself. He wept openly as he remembered how this gentle man had wrestled with whether he'd done enough.

"I'm tired of hearing this from the lips of dying people," he said. "Going to heaven is not about trying harder…. It's not about 'doing enough.' That's what grace is for. It's a free gift, and we've got to stop acting like it's something we have to earn. We can't earn it. His grace is sufficient!"

If you're growing tired and weary, it could be that you're putting your hope and trust in the wrong person—you. And 'you' will wear you out! It's often at a time like this when God can grab our attention and teach us tender truths about Himself…and His grace.

After almost thirty years of being a Christian and twenty years of marriage, God brought me to a turning point in my understanding of who He is. In 1996, after living close to family and a rich supply of friends in Nebraska for fifteen years, we moved to Atlanta. Through the many challenges we faced in Atlanta, I was gripped anew by God's amazing grace and glory.

Just the move itself was difficult—we were pulled out of our comfort zone. Immediately several situations began to unfold: our son struggled emotionally with entering a new high school; my sister, with three little boys, had a crisis in her marriage and I wasn't able to just get in the car and be there for them; and a childhood friend was diagnosed with a grave illness. These and other personal issues weighed heavily as the year progressed.

Then it was time to send our first son off to college. The pains of letting go were very real. I felt like I was losing my job, and it hurt! That same spring my dear friend died, leaving behind a husband and a young daughter. In the fall, a close uncle died. Then our son experienced heartbreak in a relationship. Things were spinning out of control—as if I ever *had* control! I was completely overwhelmed, discouraged, and spiritually depleted.

But I was a Christian! How could this be? I had been leading Bible studies for years. What was wrong? Maybe I wasn't praying hard enough or long enough or with enough faith. I was striving as hard as I knew how to be the victorious Christian woman I was supposed to be. But I was failing miserably and feeling miserable.

As a result of all of this, I began to put a lot of pressure on my husband to meet my emotional needs. He did his best, but the more I struggled, the higher I raised the bar. I was frustrated and dissatisfied. Not only did I take this out on him; I actually blamed him for how I felt!

At the same time, in His graciousness and through His Word, God opened the floodgates of His glory to me in several different ways. The people and resources He used to do this all pointed me to:

- God's sovereign grace
- God's saving grace
- God's satisfying grace

I began to realize that my understanding of almost every spiritual truth—God, salvation, prayer, living my walk—was all man-centered. I had been focusing on *my* actions, *my* feelings, *my* life story. It was all about me!

First, the eyes of my heart were opened to God's sovereignty. I began resting *in* God instead of striving *for* God. I had a deep inner peace in the midst of trying circumstances. Duty *to* God was being replaced by delight *in* God as the truth of His sovereignty began to take hold of me.

A second place of rest came as I began to understand God's saving grace. Without His grace, I am a mess! God owes me nothing but punishment and eternal condemnation, but being rich in mercy and because of His great love, I am made alive and saved, even when I was dead in my sin.[70] Salvation is from God and God alone—nothing I do "adds" to that. I contribute nothing but my sinfulness. Knowing this has set me free from striving and performing and questioning.

Michael Horton writes in *Putting Amazing Back into Grace:*

> It happens every day—whether in Los Angeles or Liverpool—no matter what the social conditions are. People undergo an internal conversion. Their views change; their disposition and interests are altered. They are suddenly at peace, experiencing the deep love of God in Christ. This event is called the new birth. It is an act of God, who tenderly and yet powerfully invades the darkness and death of the human soul, creating new life and enabling a person to respond positively in faith.[71]

I was now liberated by the truth of God's saving grace. I realized that I can have assurance because salvation is all of God from start to finish.[72]

God's satisfying grace also became a place of rest for me. I first heard John Piper, senior pastor of Bethlehem Baptist Church, speak at a conference in Atlanta. Through his books *Desiring God, Future Grace,* and *The Dangerous Duty of Delight,* he showed me that "God's passion to be glorified and my passion to be satisfied are not at odds!"[73] Christ is our "all-satisfying treasure!"

Al LaCour, my pastor, also challenged me in the area of satisfaction. One of the themes in his sermons during that time was idolatry. He said that for the unbeliever, idolatry is trying to find security and significance and satisfaction *apart from* Christ. For the believer, idolatry is trying to find security and significance and satisfaction *in addition to* Christ. Through my pastor's teaching, the Lord opened my eyes to see that I was making idols of my activities (all of those good things I was doing), even of my husband and sons and our relationships. Al gently but persistently asked the penetrating question: "Just as it is 'Christ plus nothing' for your salvation, is it 'Christ plus nothing' for your satisfaction?"

I was beginning to know deep within that my satisfaction rested in the greatness and glory of God, not the greatness and glory of anyone or anything else. In a world in which I am bombarded daily with news of evil, pain, and suffering, and in all of my weaknesses and struggles, I can rest in God's sovereign, saving, and satisfying grace. And out of the overflow of God's all-sufficient grace, I can love and respect and submit to my husband the way God intended—not perfectly, of course, but "in process." Just ask my husband if the turning point in my understanding of grace and relationship with God is the best thing that happened in our marriage—he'll say yes!

Soli Deo Gloria!

Brenda uses the acronym REST as a daily reminder to:

> R*enew my mind constantly with God's Word; look for God's attributes/character; study and dig deeply to know God intimately (Jeremiah 9:23–24; Romans 12:2; Philippians 3:7–11).*
>
> E*xpress total dependence on the Lord for the day, acknowledging and confessing sin, weaknesses, and struggles (Romans 11:33; 2 Corinthians 12:7–10; 1 John 1:8–10).*
>
> S*atisfy my heart in Christ alone! Pray Psalm 90:14 (Psalm 36:7–9; 63:5–8; Isaiah 55:1–3).*
>
> T*ake all that comes into my life as from the Lord and trust Him! My times are in His hand (Psalm 31:14–15; Isaiah 45:6–7; 46:8–10).*

Are you tired of striving and performing? Are you tired of failing miserably and feeling miserable? Stop placing your confidence in yourself, and place it in God! His grace is sufficient for you!

Are you trusting "Christ plus nothing" for your salvation and satisfaction?

Better to Live in
the Attic

...than with a Quarrelsome Wife

DEE BRESTIN

What wife would want to drive her beloved not only up the wall, but clear into the attic! If the attic was the only refuge available, we're certain that many men would rather live there than face anger—and a hurled pan! Unmet expectations combined with PMS and schedules could have made an attic dweller out of this husband—married to a woman who has become one of America's most beloved authors. As Dee was about to discover, the emptiness in her heart couldn't be completely filled by Steve. Another person is never one's source of complete joy. A husband can add to that joy, but the true source must be God Himself.

I stepped into an elevator in the Atlanta Hilton with a lovely woman. She recognized me, an unusual occurrence, so I was caught off guard when she asked, "How big a pan was it?"

"Excuse me?" I asked

"You are Dee Brestin, right?"

"Yes, but…"

"I read how you threw a pan at your husband when you were newly married."

"Oh.…" My face flushed, remembering.

"So how big a pan was it?" she asked.

I laughed, feeling like I was on candid camera.

"I just can't imagine you doing that," she persisted. "You seem so gentle. "

"Well, I wasn't so gentle before Jesus."

"Really?" she said. "Was it a skillet?"

"It was so long ago that I really don't remember. But I do remember that I missed."

"I'm glad," she said. "Your husband sounds so nice."

"Yes," I nodded. "He didn't deserve that." The elevator opened and I escaped with a smile.

As I walked toward my hotel room, I was flooded with memories. I was such a petulant and immature bride, thinking that the emptiness in my life was Steve's fault. That infamous night when I hurled a pan at him I had screamed, "You are not meeting my needs!"

Patiently he asked me what my needs were.

Tearfully I cried, "You should be able to figure that out!"

Solomon says that God has "set eternity in the hearts of men; yet they cannot fathom what God has done."[74] I had absolutely *no* idea that the longing in my heart was for a relationship with the God who made me. Instead, I blamed my husband.

So, of course, the *first* best thing I ever did for my marriage was to respond to the Good News of Jesus Christ. That happened in the second year of our marriage and was truly a pivotal moment for my life *and* for my marriage. I had a new perspective, a new power, and a new purpose. Though I now had a personal relationship with Christ, and soon after Steve did as well, I still had pain, I still had problems, and I still had PMS.

When Steve finished medical school, we moved across the country to Seattle, far from family, friends, and the church that had loved and nurtured us. Steve was doing a ninety-hour-a-week internship. He came home only to sleep. Sometimes he would try to interact with us, but he would always fall asleep on the sofa. His little boys, eager for *some* contact with their dad, would run matchbox cars up and down his legs.

As a baby Christian I cried out to Jesus for help. I wanted Him to change our circumstances—*change the internship program, change Steve's hours, change Steve!* But that isn't how the Lord answered.

On Sunday, alone in church, I read in the bulletin:

> Bible study for young moms
> Thursdays at 9:00 A.M.
> Nursery provided

I hoped someone would invite me. After all, I reasoned, I was new. Shouldn't the established people be reaching out to me?

No one stopped me after church and invited me. No one called.

So I stayed home. I was so lonely, so frustrated.

I cried out to God again. Again, I asked God to reduce Steve's long hours. When I was done praying, Steve called from the hospital. He had just seen the holiday call schedule. He was scheduled to work both Thanksgiving and Christmas. I hung up, weeping. *Lord, what kind of an answer is this?*

In the stillness I heard the clock ticking. Looking up, I

realized that the young moms would be meeting in forty minutes. Suddenly I jumped up, stuffed our little boys into their snowsuits, pushed the stroller madly up the hill, and caught the bus that would drop us near the church. After placing the boys in the warm and loving arms of the women in the nursery, I walked timidly into the room where the mothers were meeting. They had already started, but an older woman welcomed me warmly. Taking an empty chair at the big round table, I thought, *I'm just going to listen. I don't know the Bible. If I say anything, it will be stupid. I'm just going to listen.*

And I did. But at the close, an older woman said we were going to "go around the table," and each woman would share a need in her life. Then we would pray.

There was no escape.

They were coming closer and closer to me.

I was going to have to talk.

I decided I would be honest and tell them how lonely I was in Seattle. But when I tried to talk, all I could do was cry. Soon I was absolutely sobbing, blowing my nose, and feeling humiliated. *How could I be carrying on like this in front of strangers?*

I'll never forget how they responded. A few came and put their arms around me. A few prayed for me, though they could only guess at the reason for my tears. And then the invitations began to come: for lunch, for a walk around Green Lake with our kids, for tea. Some of the women seemed too old to be my friends (they were in their early thirties), but it seemed rude to refuse their invitations.

Thank God I didn't refuse. The *second* best thing I ever did for my marriage was to respond to their offers of friendship. God sent women of depth, women who helped me find strength in the God I was just beginning to know.

Lorinda invited me for tea and prayed with me, especially for Steve. As we prayed, I began to realize someone else in this marriage was hurting. Steve was trying to survive the hardest year of his life, trying *not* to sink under the swirling waves. Was I helping him survive? No! I was another weight dragging him down.

Patti and I would walk around Green Lake pushing strollers. With humor she quoted proverbs about quarrelling wives, telling me how they had convicted *her*. I remember she told me that whenever there was a problem between her and her husband, that if she got things right with God, usually the problem between her and her husband ironed out as well. I've never forgotten that truth.

Bea opened her home to all of us, where we would congregate with our children, laugh, pray, and help one another find strength in God. Slowly I was gaining strength, so that I, in turn, could throw Steve a lifeline.

We made it through that year, and through the next thirty-five years of marriage. I don't know when we crossed over from the "wilderness" years to the "invincible" love years—but it was so long ago, I can't remember. I do know that by the time I reached *my* thirties that God was using me to throw a lifeline to younger women, helping *them* find strength in God.

I've often been inspired by the story of Mary and Elizabeth—how Mary was alert to seek out a woman of depth, and how Elizabeth gave generously of herself, helping Mary prepare for what was going to be a challenging road ahead. I find myself in both roles: always looking for women of depth—not just believers, but believers who are living lives of radical obedience; I also want to always be open to the younger women in my life, and to give generously, helping them become the women God intended them to be.

After Dee made a commitment to Christ, her eyes were opened to see that women need the friendship of other women! How draining for a husband to feel like his wife's only friend. He should certainly be her best friend, but we're wired so differently! It's not unusual for a woman to go on and on sharing each and every detail of a story, much to her girlfriend's delight. Yet for the most part, men want only the bottom line. Dee had three precious friends who acted as trustworthy sounding boards. They not only encouraged her but also exhorted her about her marriage, which prepared Dee at a very young age to help other young women understand God's plan for them. Now thousands of women have been mentored by Dee's wisdom, as shared in her numerous books. Isn't it amazing how God allows the "trouble" a person faces to become her "pulpit" for helping others?

You can find out more about Dee Brestin on her website at DeeBrestin.com. She is the author of The Friendships of Women *and coauthor, with Kathy Troccoli, of* Falling in Love with Jesus. *She is also the mother-in-law of Julie Brestin, whom Dee describes as "your dream daughter-in-law" and also has a chapter in this book.*

What younger women in your sphere of influence could you approach as a mentor? If you're in need of a mentor, ask God to point her out to you.

When You Know
the King
...Everything Changes!

KAY OSIKA

For many years, one of the most powerful ministries in the Midwest has been a Bible study taught by Kay Osika. Her influence has surely spread throughout the world because she has taught thousands of women the truths revealed in God's Word. There is absolutely no way that her ministry would have had such impact had she not chosen to become a godly wife. Both of our lives have been touched by her ministry, and we know why. Kay knows the King!

My husband and I recently celebrated our thirty-sixth wedding anniversary. The number of years we have been married surprises me, but the fact that we are still married does not, for we began our marriage with the belief that it was for life and nothing but death would end it. That view might seem old-fashioned in today's culture but it is a value my husband and I had been taught by our parents and our church. It has

246

held us together through difficult times. But it isn't just our belief—it is God's truth.

As a young child I used to play with a dollhouse. I could move the furniture and even the little people wherever I wanted them to go. Day after day I would arrange the chairs, beds, tables, and dishes. The people also moved to my whim. In the early years of our marriage, I often behaved as if I were still playing house and everyone, including my husband, was to conform to my expectations. This childish way of thinking did not make for a happy home: "Take out the trash! Mow the lawn! Dress up! Be what I want you to be! Make me happy!" A grown man isn't moved as easily as a dollhouse toy. And a grown woman isn't supposed to play with dolls!

God was aware of my need to grow up, so He took me through several stretching circumstances. We moved often during the first six years of our marriage, six times exactly. This involved six homes to arrange and then, just as quickly, take apart. Also, our four children were born during this time. I remember being tired and frustrated because my world had become quite unmanageable. All four kids required attention and energy. Sleep became far more appealing than spending time with my husband. We stopped communicating except about the necessities.

Then one day God brought Mary Anne into my life. Whenever we were together, she made herself available to listen to me. She understood my complaints, but she didn't stop with just listening. She offered a solution. "Come to a Bible study!"

"Bible study? No way!"

What I needed (or so I thought) was a course in the male psyche and the ways of a strong-willed child. But Mary Anne was persistent. After two years of friendship and observing her with her children and receiving the benefits of her kindness, I agreed to go to the study. My motives, however, were not pure. Mary Anne had said that there would be something for the children as well. This sounded like a "moms' day out," so I was eager to go if only for a short break from my children. What a surprise awaited me! This study was the beginning of a change not only for me but for our marriage as well.

One day as I was reading about Jesus in Colossians, all that I knew about Him suddenly came into focus. It was as if someone had adjusted the lens on a fuzzy telescope and I could see clearly that Jesus had died for my sins so that I could come into a right relationship with the holy God of the universe. The Bible said that He is the image of the invisible God, the firstborn over all creation, before all things, and He holds all things together, and that all God's fullness dwells in Jesus. He is the one who reconciled all things to Himself, making peace through His blood shed on the cross. As I read, I knew that He had done it for me! The words kept speaking to me! Christ is the reconciler between me and God. He would present me to God without blemish. I would be free from accusation if I would believe Him and not move away from the hope held out in the gospel.[75] That very hour I committed myself to Jesus Christ and gave up what I thought was my right to run my life.

My husband began to notice a change in me. No longer was I the starter of arguments. I began to focus on grateful thoughts instead of shouting demanding words. I treated him with respect. As I did this my expectations of what a happy marriage should look like changed. No longer was I the mover of people and furniture. Now I was a woman dependent on the grace of God and His love for me. I learned to call on the Lord for wisdom when I didn't know how to respond to my husband or children.[76] I needed to rethink all of my expectations regarding marriage from a new perspective—God's![77]

Reading the Bible and applying these truths to my life caused me to hope in God and trust His ways.[78] My self-centered ambitions for my life were replaced with the promises of God Himself.[79]

Who could ask for more?

An elderly woman recently told us, "There's nothing worse than getting to the end of your life and having so many regrets." She was eighty years old and the regrets she was referring to had to do with the way she'd treated her husband for the better part of sixty years. He died unexpectedly—how she wishes she could go back and start afresh.

You can! Don't allow the crayon of regret to be the primary color when you come to life's end. Start today to do what God has called you to do. Need a shot of adrenalin to get you started? Here's one for you: "Strip down, start running—and never quit! No extra spiritual fat, no parasitic sins. Keep your eyes on Jesus…"[80]

Keep your eyes on Jesus! That's what keeps Kay going…and that's what will keep you going as well. When you serve your husband, you serve the King of kings and Lord of lords.

Keep going, dear friend. Keep going.…

Are you keeping your eyes on Jesus as you stay the course?

Where You Don't Want to Live

The Back Burner

"Stay Right There. I'll Check Back
on You in Nineteen Years."

ANONYMOUS

*H*ow do we get sidetracked as wives? Is it children? Surely they can keep a woman hopping. Is it ministry? If it is, doesn't that seem like a good and holy reason? Is it a career? She goes to work, comes home and works—where can she find the time and energy to invest in her husband? Or the desire? Isn't he absorbed in his career as well? Why is it always put on a wife to keep the home fires burning? Well, the answer to the last question is, it isn't! But since this is a book for women, and since you are 100 percent responsible for the way you live your life before God, let's examine the front and back burners of your relational life.

Marcy Wilson[81] is a close friend of mine (Nancy). Anyone would say she "has it all." She has unbelievable children, prosperity, a second home, an influential ministry, and a well-known husband. She is beautiful as well—bright, with a sunny disposition. She loves the Lord and serves Him in her ministry…but what about in her home?

I met Marcy on a retreat. Neither of us wanted a roommate because we were both weary. But having that in common caused us *to stay up most of the night talking! I sent her an invitation to write a chapter for this book, and my admiration for her grew when I saw her integrity through her story. Marcy did some soul searching and discovered, to her amazement, that she had long ago put her husband on the back burner.*

Maybe you've done this as well. If you have, you're going to appreciate and admire Marcy's honesty. Perhaps her story will catapult you into taking a long look at the burners of your own life and seeing if there aren't some things that need changing. Marcy's story is below:

Dear Nancy,

I have waited to write this note, hoping I would find time to write a chapter for your book, but I am sorry to say I do not have one. It was amazing…as the Bible study I was teaching finally finished around the end of May, I began to think about what I would write. The Lord put upon my heart that for eighteen years I have been giving my all to ministry, but I have been giving my husband the leftovers.

Often, during the summer months, I travel to the mountains just to relax and enjoy the mountain air. This summer, I knew I should not leave my husband and that I must give him my whole-hearted devotion and attention. So the best thing I can do for my marriage is not to get all wrapped up in writing a chapter, but to work on loving my husband with everything I have. I have found that I take him for granted. One day his secretary said to me, "It is a privilege to work for such a godly man." I thought, *I never seem to see him like that and it is about time that I did. I had better appreciate him more and think less of myself!*

Do you see, Nancy? I must work on making my marriage the best it can be, which I know is what you and Connie are constantly teaching. I am continuing to pray for you and consider it a privilege to do so. Please forgive me for not submitting a chapter, but thank you for even thinking of me. Because you gave me an opportunity to think about this, I am a more appreciative wife!

Marcy's story is all too common. The question is: Would her fruitfulness increase if she invested her time and energy more in her husband than in outside ministry? Only God knows, but Marcy is well on her way to finding out!

What is unusual is that when Marcy realized what she had done, she was not only challenged to do something about it, but was also willing to admit it. She could easily have said that she didn't have time, or was taking the summer off, but she didn't. I called her as soon as I read her note and asked if we could use her story just as she had written it as our epilogue. She humbly said yes.

Marcy can't possibly be the only one who has set aside her first ministry. Have you? The thing we so often fail to realize is that when we serve our husbands in Jesus' name, He considers Himself the one served. This changes everything! Every motive becomes pure, every duty becomes sweet, and every act becomes holy.

When you commit to living this way, your life will never be the same. Your earthly life will be changed, but even better, a day will come when you'll be able to stand before your Maker confident and unashamed.

So won't you, right now, consider asking God to help you get your wife life back on track? And if it's on track, ask Him to help you keep it on track and make it more glorifying to Him than ever before.

We thought it would be fitting to end this book with our paraphrase of Matthew 25:35–40:

I was hungry for breakfast, dinner, and sometimes even lunch, snacks,
a kind word, a warm hug, to talk to you, to be loved by you....
You gave me something to eat.
I was thirsty to feel accepted by you,
I mowed the lawn and needed refreshing and...
you gave me something to drink.
I was a stranger; my mood was bad. I had been unreasonable.
I had been mean, thoughtless, forgetful, unhelpful, self-centered....
You invited me in.
I was naked; you did all my wash, even when I dropped it on the floor.
You sewed on my missing buttons.
You ironed my wrinkled shirts.
You let me bare my soul to you.
You saw the real me that others never see—
with all my quirks and uncovered ugliness,
and you never exposed me before our children, family, or friends....
You clothed me.
I was sick—you know my colds are worse than anyone else's.
Sometimes I said things I didn't mean. I got depressed and...
you cared for me.
I was in prison: My job got to me some days and I withdrew from you.
When I was lonely you were there for me. You prayed for me.
When I was consumed with a problem, when I was unforgiving,
when I didn't deserve anything because of the way
I've treated you and I was so ashamed...
you came to me.
Jesus would say to you,
"When you did these things for your husband,
you did them for Me."

Our life on earth has been compared to a race.[82] One day the race will end, and you'll fall into the arms of your Father. Imagine Him looking into your eyes, a smile crossing His face, as He says, "What you did for your husband never went unnoticed. Your words…your actions…your attitudes…your forgiving heart. I saw everything and took special note. Well done, my child, well done! You were faithful to the end!"

Surely there are no sweeter words. So start running! Keep running! And don't stop…until you fall into the arms of the precious One who loves you most.

God bless you!

Notes

1. Galatians 5:22–23.
2. Isaiah 54:5–8.
3. Romans 12:2.
4. Genesis 2:18.
5. Genesis 2:18. This is the primary "job description" for a wife.
6. 1 Peter 3:4.
7. Patrick M. Morley, *What Husbands Wish Their Wives Knew About Men* (Grand Rapids, Mich.: Zondervan, 1997), 172–3.
8. Ibid., 177.
9. Ephesians 5:25.
10. Luke 6:38; 2 Corinthians 9:6; Galatians 6:7.
11. Luke 6:35, paraphrased.
12. John 20:29.
13. Proverbs 31:11.
14. Song quote from *Mr. Rogers' Neighborhood* TV Show.
15. See Ephesians 2:10.
16. Dina Maria Mulock Craik, *A Life for a Life* (London: Collins' Clear Type Press, 1900), taken from Hazel Felleman, ed., *The Best Loved Poems of the American People* (New York: Garden City Books, 1936).
17. Romans 14:4, 10, 13, NASB, emphasis added.
18. Dr. Gary Chapman, *The Five Love Languages* (Chicago, Ill.: Northfield Publishing, 1992).
19. Charles R. Swindoll, *Strike the Original Match* (Portland, Oreg.: Multnomah Press, 1980), 59.
20. John 19:27.
21. Matthew 5:46, 48, *The Message*.
22. Thomas O. Chisolm, "O to Be Like Thee!" 1897. Music by William J. Kirkpatrick.
23. Proverbs 14:1.
24. Matthew 6:33.
25. Psalm 37:8.
26. As quoted in Dr. Joe White, *Life Training: Devotions for Parents and Teens* (Wheaton, Ill.: Tyndale, 1998), 205.
27. Ezekiel 11:19; 36:26.

28. 1 Peter 3:8.
29. Revelation 2:2–5.
30. Ephesians 5:33, AMP.
31. Romans 12:2.
32. Ephesians 5:33, AMP.
33. Luke 6:33–36, paraphrased.
34. Matthew 19:9.
35. Matthew 6:14–15.
36. Psalm 91:2.
37. See John 15.
38. Matthew 25:34–40.
39. Luke 6:27–36.
40. Matthew 18:21–35; Luke 6:37–38.
41. Psalm 46:10.
42. Romans 8:28.
43. Revelation 22:16.
44. Romans 12:17–21.
45. Matthew 25:21.
46. Isaiah 26:3, paraphrased.
47. Jeremiah 29:11.
48. Matthew 6:14–15, paraphrased.
49. Matthew 6:14.
50. 2 Corinthians 3:18.
51. Ruth Myers, *31 Days of Praise* (Sisters, Oreg.: Multnomah, 2002).
52. 2 Chronicles 20:15, AMP.
53. John Finley hand delivered his wife's story to me.
54. 1 Corinthians 7:4.
55. 1 Corinthians 7:2–6, *The Message*.
56. Genesis 2:25.
57. Genesis 2:18.
58. Colossians 3:18, AMP. See also Ephesians 5:22.
59. William E. Barton, *Safed the Sage* (Louisville, Ky.: Westminster John Knox, 1983).
60. James 1:5.
61. Proverbs 21:1; Matthew 7:7–8.
62. Psalm 65:5.
63. Psalm 101:2.
64. Matthew 7:12.

65. 1 Corinthians 13:13.
66. John 3:16.
67. Proverbs 14:1.
68. 2 Timothy 3:15.
69. Psalm 127:1.
70. Ephesians 2:4–5.
71. Michael S. Horton, *Putting Amazing Back into Grace*, 2nd ed. (Grand Rapids, Mich.: Baker, 2002), 248.
72. Philippians 1:6.
73. John Piper, *The Dangerous Duty of Delight* (Sisters, Oreg.: Multnomah, 2001), 20.
74. Ecclesiastes 3:11.
75. Colossians 1:15–23.
76. Psalm 119:66.
77. Psalm 119:73.
78. Romans 15:4.
79. Psalm 130:5.
80. Hebrews 12:1–2, *The Message*.
81. A pseudonym.
82. 2 Timothy 4:6–8. See also Acts 20:24.

STUCK IN UNHOLY DEADLOCK? SO WERE WE...

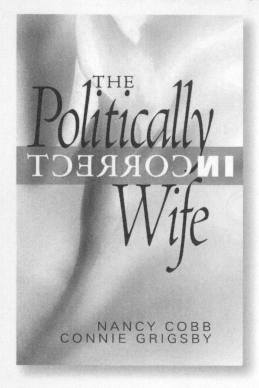

Speak Your Husband's Language: Male!

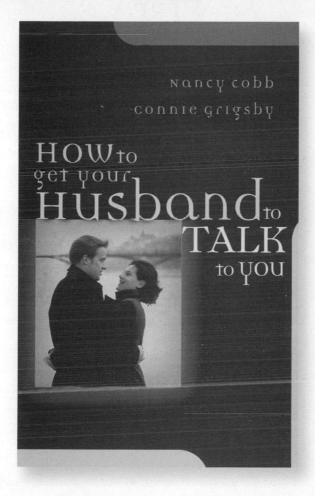

Two women's ministries leaders have collaborated on a primer that promises to resolve the age-old mystery of communication between the sexes—and leave men and women conversing happily. Cobb and Grigsby present a five-step "training program" for women who choose to love their husbands more effectively, but need practical help learning the best approach. Chapters on loving, learning, listening, loyalty, and laughter guide a wife up five levels of essential skills to promote unity, trust, and friendship with the man whose company she most enjoys and desires.

ISBN 1-57673-771-3